ON THE SHADOWS OF THE IDEAS

On the Shadows of the Ideas

*Comprising an art of investigating,
discovering, judging, ordering, and applying,
set forth for the purpose of inner writing, and
not for vulgar operations of memory*

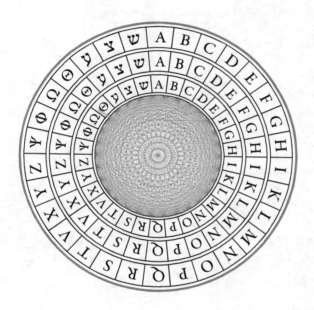

Giordano Bruno

Translated from the Latin by
John Michael Greer

AZOTH
PRESS™

2020

First Paperback Edition
published 2020 Azoth Press
ISBN 978-1-935006-97-8

First Limited Hardcover Edition
published 2017 Azoth Press

Azoth Press
Portland, OR
USA
www.azothpress.com

Contents

List of Illustrations

The Magical Images also include 19 woodcuts of the Signs and Planets
from the early Latin editions
of the works of Bruno.

✟

Translator's Preface

IORDANO BRUNO is a tolerably famous figure in contemporary culture, a subject of popular biographies and histories, and a minor saint in the pantheon of contemporary rationalism. His Italian dialogues have all long since been translated into English and have their assigned places in an assortment of university curricula, and it's a rare survey of the late Renaissance that doesn't spare him a place. It's therefore remarkable, to use no stronger word, that the body of his work that Bruno himself considered most important—the development of a method for encyclopedic knowledge, combining philosophy and mnemotechnics—has been so generally neglected by the world of modern scholarship.

Of course there are reasons for that neglect. As Paolo Rossi pointed out many years ago in *Logic and the Art of Memory*, the quest for a *pansophia*, a universal method of knowledge, that exercised so many of the great minds of the Renaissance was excised from Western intellectual culture over the course of the eighteenth century, and the harsh polemics directed at the old pansophic vision by the standardbearers of the soi-disant Age of Reason are still accepted at face value by a remarkably broad range of scholars and intellectuals today.[1] The world of modern thought, it bears remembering, was built atop the ruins of Renaissance thinking—and a great many of the ruins in question were still standing, and indeed occupied, when the wrecking crews of early modern rationalism pulled them down.

The vision that guided the pansophists of the Renaissance was as simple as it was ambitious. Looking upon the available knowledge of their time, they

---

1. Rossi 2000, pp. xv–xx.

saw a jumble of disparate fields, each of which had a more or less ramshackle body of traditional theory balanced unsteadily atop a mass of poorly correlated facts. Their quest—the same quest that inspired Francis Bacon's quest for a "great instauration" and ultimately resulted in the emergence of the modern scientific method—was for a single method that would allow all knowledge to be brought together, compared, correlated, and used to generate new bodies of knowledge. The tools they hoped to use for this task included two sciences that have all but vanished from the landscape of contemporary thought: the art of memory, a traditional system of mnemotechnics dating from classical times, and the art of combinations or Lullian art, an algebra of abstract concepts devised in the Middle Ages.

On the Shadows of the Ideas was Bruno's major published contribution to the Renaissance quest for a universal method of knowledge. Most of the text deals with the mnemotechnical side of his work, and stands to this day as the high-water mark of the Renaissance art of memory; other elements clearly derive from the Lullian art. The fusion of these two currents in Bruno's mind gave rise to a broader practice, not limited to "vulgar operations of memory"—a method of "inner writing" meant, as Bruno indicates in his text, for investigating, discovering, judging, ordering, and applying ideas. The nature of that art can be understood, and its methods partly reconstructed, by reviewing the broader context of Bruno's own life and work.

The Man

Bruno was born in 1548 in the little southern Italian town of Nola, the son of a soldier and his peasant wife. He entered the Dominican order as a novice in 1565 and took final vows in the following year. He studied for the priesthood at the College of San Domenico Maggiore in Naples, one of the leading theological centers of the time, and also found time to study Plato's philosophy with the Augustinian monks of the monastery of St. Giovanni a Carbonara. It was his teacher at the latter, Fra Teofilo da Vairano, who introduced him to the magical Platonism of Marsilio Ficino, the great Florentine scholar who revived Hermeticism for the Renaissance with his Latin translation of the Corpus Hermeticum; it was his Dominican teachers who introduced him to the art of memory and the Lullian art of combinations, the two mental disciplines that he would fuse into a vehicle for his work. All three of these currents are obscure enough to most modern readers that they deserve some discussion here.

The art of memory was almost completely forgotten in the Western world when the late Frances Yates reintroduced it to historians in her justly famous 1966 book. Invented in ancient Greece, it was widely used by orators in the Classical world, and was recovered from Latin texts in the Middle Ages. Practitioners memorized the insides of suitable building, and stocked them in imagination with symbolic images meant to recall either things or words to memory. Odd though this seems to the modern mind, it works; readers who doubt this are invited to test the simplified method introduced in the practical guide that follows the translation.

In the wake of its medieval resurrection, the art of memory became a common practice among clergy, especially among members of preaching orders such as the Dominicans, who used it to facilitate extempore sermons. Bruno was introduced to it as a matter of course in his monastic training, and became so expert at the art that in 1569 his superiors in the Dominican Order sent him to Rome to display his skills to the Pope.

The Lullian art, or *ars combinatoria*, has not received the same level of attention from modern scholars as the Art of Memory, though it is not quite as obscure as it was before Yates' time.[2] Created by the thirteenth-century Catalan mystic Ramon Lull, and strongly influenced by the earliest forms of the Cabala, the Lullian art was a system of conceptual algebra that promised to solve all philosophical problems. Lull began with nine "dignities" or fundamental concepts— goodness, greatness, duration, power, wisdom, will, virtue, truth, and glory—each of which has its own definition, and which are combined with each other in various formal ways.

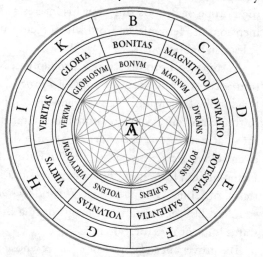

Fig. 1. A sample of a nine-category Lullian wheel (after Bruno, ON THE ARCHITECTURE OF THE ART OF LULL)

2. The most useful and accessible materials on Lull currently known to me are provided by Dr. Yanis Dambergs, a contemporary practitioner of the tradition, at http://www.lullianarts. narpan.net.

In the standard Lullian system, there are also nine relative terms—difference, concord, contrariety, beginning, middle, end, majority, equality, and minority—as well as nine levels of being, nine virtues, nine vices, and ten questions. Each of these were assigned to nested wheels, either on paper or in the imagination, which could be turned freely to ask each question of each combination of concepts. According to Lull, a trained practitioner of his system could move from the definitions to conclusions infallibly and provide clear answers to any theological or philosophical question.

The Lullian art was a subject of great interest, and also great controversy, all through Bruno's life. Alongside the basic method presented by Lull, there were various expansions and revisions, many of which sought to integrate it with the art of memory into a comprehensive method that would allow all human knowledge to be synthesized and grasped by a single mind. Such grand projects as the memory theater of Giulio Camillo unfolded from this ambition—and so did the grand project of Bruno's that took shape in *On the Shadows of the Ideas*.

As already noted, though, a more secretive tradition also flowed into Bruno's work. He knew his way around the Renaissance Hermeticism of Marsilio Ficino and Giovanni Pico de Mirandola, which had a massive intellectual presence in the Europe of Bruno's time, but his interests also extended into the occult dimensions of Hermeticism from which Ficino and Pico both piously recoiled—at least in public.

At some point in his studies, probably in Naples, someone unnamed gave him access to a manuscript copy of *Picatrix*, the most notorious magician's handbook of the Middle Ages. Originally composed in Muslim Spain sometime in the tenth century by an anonymous Arab sorcerer, *Picatrix* was translated into Latin in 1256 at the court of Alfonso the Wise, King of Castile, and was circulated in secret among occultists in Europe for centuries thereafter. Marsilio Ficino quoted from it in his writings, without naming his source. So did Heinrich Cornelius Agrippa, whose *Three Books of Occult Philosophy* became the standard European primer of magic during Bruno's lifetime and retained that status for centuries thereafter.

The provenance of copies of *Picatrix* whose owners can be traced reads like a who's who of prominent wizards—for example, a single copy in 16th and 17th century England was owned in turn by three of the most famous occultists of the age, the sorcerer Simon Forman, the alchemist Elias Ashmole, and the astrologer William Lilly. Where Bruno got his copy is unknown, but many of the magical images included in *On the Shadows of the Ideas* come straight from the pages of *Picatrix*.

At the time, certainly, a taste in reading that included *Picatrix* did not augur well for Bruno's orthodoxy, and in fact he had already come to the attention of the Inquisition in Naples before he took final vows as a Dominican. In 1576, the Inquisition began a new investigation into his beliefs and activities, and was able to document that he had been reading books banned by the Church. Fearing excommunication or worse, Bruno fled to Rome, and then left Italy and the Dominican order altogether.

He spent most of the remainder of his life traveling from city to city and country to country across most of Europe, stopping for a year or two to lecture and try to attract disciples, and then moving on. He dabbled in espionage in England and elsewhere, and wrote a number of elegant dialogues on philosophical themes and a raucous comic play titled *Candelaio*. Mostly, however, he taught a discipline all his own, one that combined the art of memory and Lull's art of combinations with a magical subtext derived from *Picatrix*, and used the whole as a system by which all human knowledge could be mastered and put to work.

This art was originally created sometime before 1582, when *On the Shadows of the Ideas* first saw print, and was described in complete form only in the pages of a book that does not survive, the *Clavis Magna* or "*Great Key.*" That hidden art provides, however, the framework on which each of his major works on the art of memory were written. From those latter works, some aspect of the underlying system can be learned, but other dimensions of it remain a mystery to this day.

The system of the *Clavis Magna* was the teaching he passed on to students in his travels, passing them on to the Scots mnemonist Alexander Dicson and—if the Roman Inquisition is to be believed—to secret circles of "*Giordanisti*" in Germany. The acclaim he hoped to win for his mnemonic inventions never came, though, and his attempts to find a patron who would support him turned out to be his undoing. In 1591 a Venetian nobleman, Zuan Mocenigo, hired him as an instructor and, after quarreling with him, turned him over to the Church. The Inquisition was not interested in his mnemonic system; they were interested instead in his heresies, which were considerable, and duly burnt him at the stake at Rome in 1600.

The Book

On the Shadows of the Ideas, Bruno's first publication, is not a user-friendly book, and Bruno never intended it to be one. He wrote it for the educated elite of Renaissance Europe, convinced that they would recognize the value of his discoveries and give him the fame and wealth he craved. Thus he filled its pages with erudite Latin poems, Classical allusions, and deliberate obscurities that make it hard going for the modern reader, and were apparently not much easier at the time Bruno wrote.

Bruno's own introductions are of a piece with the intricate work that follows them. An initial poem, "To the Friendly and Studious Reader," uses two famous classical stories to suggest that the difficult process of struggling through *On the Shadows of the Ideas*, and making sense of its contents, will be richly repaid. The letter of dedication to Henri III of France, the book's patron, mixes flattery with Bruno's usual arrogance; so great a gift as *On the Shadows of the Ideas*, he suggests, must be dedicated to the greatest of kings.

Thereafter come three riddling poems that Bruno puts in the mouth of Merlin, the great enchanter of Arthurian legend, who had a Europe-wide reputation in the Renaissance. The first, "Merlin to the Artist," expands on the dedication's flattery by suggesting that so splendid a portrayal of the French king may land Bruno in trouble. The second, "Merlin to the Judges, on Sobriety," warns teasingly that more than a little attention to the book may drive the reader "headlong to madness or glory;" considering Bruno's own fate, this may be considered uncomfortably prophetic.

The last, "Merlin to the Judges, on Appropriateness," argues that the art of memory is not opposed to nature, as some of its contemporary critics suggested, but warns readers that they are venturing into a labyrinth without a guiding thread. In a foreshadowing of Bruno's own memory techniques, a chain of shared words and images turn these poems into stepping-stones that take the reader from the dedication preceding them to the preliminary dialogue that follows.

This dialogue shows Bruno at the height of his literary powers—lively, rude, satirical, and consistently funny, without ever letting his humor get in the way of his argument. The dialogue starts with Hermes Trismegistus himself reading aloud from Bruno's book, trying to decide if it's worth publishing or not. Philothimus, whose name means "Lover of Courage," urges Hermes to send it out into the world even if nobody reads it, and ends up debating the point with Logifer, "Word-Bearer," whose name puns on "Lucifer" and who plays the part by imitating Satan's role from the Book of Job. Logifer sets out to show that Bruno's book is doomed to fail by quoting all the standard arguments against the art of memory, putting them into the mouths of imaginary experts with preposterous names—"Doctor Idiot," "Master Enema," and so on. Philothimus responds to each of these expert opinions with witty insults that also, and surely not by accident, assign clear memory images to each argument. As the debate winds down, Logifer and Philothimus ask Hermes to read more from the book, and the dialogue flows seamlessly into Bruno's own prologue, in which he explains the philosophical roots of his system and outlines the contents of the book.

The book itself, as Bruno explains, falls into two parts. The second part, the mnemonic system that occupies most of the book, is presented in relatively straightforward terms, though even so it is perhaps the most intricate mnemonic system ever to come out of the art of memory. The first is far more obscurely defined: an art of writing internally that may be used for investigating, discovering, judging, ordering, and applying knowledge, as a method that can be applied to all the operations of the mind, and as the source of a great many methods, of which the art of memory is only one. Bruno stresses that this higher dimension of his book is difficult to learn, and should be kept secret by those few who are able to master it.

Accordingly, *On the Shadows of the Ideas* never explains exactly how to practice the higher dimension—though it's by no means impossible to figure out at least some of the meaning behind his portentous hints. For example, it's clear from material covered in the first chapter of "On the Art of Memory" that one of the foundations of his art is a single memory image into which all others are placed, and that this image is probably a representation of the universe. This is far from unique in the art of memory; the famous classical Greek mnemonist Metrodorus of Scepsis was said to use a memory system based on the 360 degrees of the zodiac, and Metrodorus' example was much cited by authors on mnemotechnics before and during Bruno's time.

Most likely, Bruno's core memory image is the circle of the zodiac divided into its terms—subdivisions of the zodiacal signs, five to each sign. Traditional instructions in the art of memory in Bruno's time, and for centuries beforehand, taught the practitioner to divide the imaginary "places" used to hold memory images into groups of five, so the assignment of five places to each sign of the zodiac was not particularly novel. What made Bruno's system distinctive was that he combined it with the wheels of the Lullian art, assigning a basic concept to each of the sixty terms.

Based on the material in *On the Shadows of the Ideas*, there were thirty basic concepts from Platonic philosophy, and thirty more from Aristotelian philosophy; the first set will have gone into the terms from the beginning of Aries and the end of Virgo, the bright half of the year corresponding to the light of the Ideas, and the second set into the terms from the beginning of Libra to the end of Pisces, the dark half of the year corresponding to the shadows of material existence. In all probability, Bruno took his sixty concepts from the introductory works he studied during his monastic training, but I lack the familiarity with sixteenth-century Italian philosophical pedagogy to guess what the specific concepts might have been.

The two chapters "Thirty Intentions of the Shadows" and "Thirty Conceptions of the Ideas" comprise Bruno's closest approach to a clear discussion of the system of the *Clavis Magna*. On display here is the Lullian side of that system, using nested wheels of thirty Intentions and thirty Conceptions, in place of Lull's nine dignities and nine relative terms. Instead of listing the Intentions and Conceptions, what he provides in *On the Shadows of the Ideas* are the products of his method, the first created by applying his Intentions to the concept of shadow and the principles of Aristotelian philosophy, the second created by applying his Conceptions to the concept of light and the principles of Platonic philosophy. I have not attempted to work out these details of Bruno's system, leaving it—as Bruno left it—to the reader's own insights and imagination.

The art of memory that follows is far more explicitly presented. Here again, to be sure, he is concerned with winning the approval of the educated elite of his time, and so much of what is covered in the first of the three chapters titled "On the Art of Memory" is meant to situate his mnemonic techniques in the context of the Renaissance philosophy of mind and memory. This will mostly be of interest to students of the history of ideas. The second chapter explores the basic concepts of his art in more detail; the third presents the practical mnemonic method in outline. Further on come the long lists of mnemonic images, and after these comes a long chapter on the use of the art. Here he discusses the practical application of his mnemonics, and it's here that the method itself is described in sufficient completeness that the modern practitioner can readily put it to use.

His system derives from older mnemotechnics but expands on that tradition in unique ways. In place of the places and figures of the classic art of memory,

Bruno uses subjects and adjects. The first are images of any kind—which can be places, though they don't have to be—which are linked to one another in a specific sequence, so that each of them calls the next to mind. The latter are other images that can be added to the first set to give them their mnemonic content. For example, a human figure of some memorable nature can be a subject, and can be decked out in the imagination with a hat, clothes, weapons, tools, jewelry, or the like as adjects. The subject keeps the material in order, the adject contains the memorized content.

A significant theme of the book is the challenge, much discussed and debated in Renaissance mnemonic circles, of memorizing text verbatim. Here Bruno's methods are well in advance of any other published mnemonic system known to me. He uses images to represent pairs of letters rather than individual letters, cutting the total number of images needed nearly in half, and supplies a variety of useful tricks to make one image serve for two—for example, as he points out, a figure can stand for one pair of letters (say, MA) when imagined standing, and the reverse (AM) when seated. The flexibility of his system of subjects and adjects makes it easier for the experienced user to string images together in sequence, memorizing textual material quickly and recalling it just as quickly.

It's worth noting that Bruno's system is primarily suited to memorizing texts in Latin, though he adds seven additional letters—four Greek and three Hebrew—to expand his system to work with those languages as well. Most Latin words are made of consonant-vowel pairs, with three consonants (L, M, and R) that can be inserted into the middle of a word, and eleven that can be put on the end. The same principle is somewhat more difficult to apply to English, which does not always break apart so neatly into consonant-vowel pairs; consider the word "English" itself, with its flurry of additional consonants. (On the other hand, there are languages—Japanese is one—that are even better suited to Bruno's method than Latin, being even more strictly based on consonant-vowel pairs.)

Many pages of *On the Shadows of the Ideas* are devoted to long lists of images that correspond to consonant–vowel pairs of the sort just described. Most of these are harmless by the standards of the time, if eccentric—the list of 150 legendary inventors from Rhegima, who figured out how to make bread from chestnuts, through Simonides of Melos, who invented the art of memory, is a good example—but a significant fraction were not. Magical images of the planets, zodiacal signs, and mansions of the moon play a significant role in the magic of *Picatrix*, and since Bruno himself wrote essays on the practice of magic, it's tolerably clear that he knew exactly what he was doing when he included these images.

Exactly why he did so is a complex matter. In the Renaissance magical theory Bruno knew well, magical images impressed on any substance—including the human imagination—call down forces from the heavens into manifestation on earth. Using such images for purely mnemonic purposes, according to the same theory, would risk unwelcome consequences, especially if that was done at a time when the planet ruling an image was badly placed, when the sign or mansion of the moon ruling an image had a malefic planet in it, or some similar debility.

Far more likely is that Bruno meant the images to be used to enhance the memory by means of magic, and a method for doing so will be discussed in the practical guide following the text.

Another question that may be worth exploring is whether Bruno also meant his system as a means of cryptography. As mentioned above, Bruno dabbled in espionage during his years of wandering about Europe, and the boundary between occult philosophy and secret writing had been extremely porous since the fifteenth-century mage Johannes Trithemius wrote the *Steganographia*, a manual of ciphers that concealed secret messages under the appearance of magical incantations. It would not have been at all out of character for Bruno to have included a similar scheme in his all-embracing system.

The detail of Bruno's system that makes it suitable as a system of cryptography is that the inventors, adjectives, and the like don't relate to the alphabet in the most useful way—by having the first two letters of the name of the symbol be the letter combination for which it stands. That would have been easy enough to do: Aaron for AA, Aeneas for AE, and so on, would have been straightforward to create and easy to memorize and use. Instead, Bruno gives Rhegima for AA, Osiris for AE, and so on. That's harder to memorize and use—but by the same token, a bit of allegorical poetry that had Hasamon transplanting a tree and Baros making brass strings would spell out, to the adept in Bruno's system, CAVE—"beware."

None of these details make Bruno's method particularly easy on the beginner, and Bruno himself offers several simplified methods for novices at the end of his book. These place the subjects and adjects in a set of predetermined places, such as the twelve houses of the astrological chart, so that the practitioner can get used to the extraordinary wealth of images in Bruno's system while still memorizing things in what, at the time, was the familiar way.

All in all, *On the Shadows of the Ideas* is an extraordinary work of Renaissance literature, occultism, and mnemonic theory and practice. It has been an education, as well as a pleasure, to translate it into English.

John Michael Greer

✢

Author's Introductions

PH. GIORD. BR. NOL.[1]
To the Friendly and Studious Reader.

It is set up high,
  The face of Diana in Chios
  That seems sorrowful to those who enter her temple
  But looks joyful to those who leave it.[2]

And the letter of Pythagoras,
  Dividing action into two paths,[3]
  While it shows a forbidding face to those who choose the right,
  Bestows on them the highest good.

That which rises from the profound
  Darkness of the shadows
  Will be welcome in the end, though more bitter now
  Than the face or the letter.

---

1. PH. GIORD. BR. NOL.: Represents PH. IORD. BR. NOL. in the original Latin, an abbreviation for *Philotheus Iordanus Brunus Nolanus*: "Philotheus (Greek Φιλόθεος, 'God-loving') Giordano Bruno the Nolan."

2. A famous statue of Diana on Chios was said to have this visual effect.

3. The Greek letter Υ in Pythagorean lore represents the choice between virtue and vice; the righthand fork of virtue was covered with barbs and thorns but led to happiness.

TO HIS SERENE MAJESTY, HENRI III, KING OF FRANCE AND POLAND, ETC.
Philotheus Jordanus Brunus Nolanus offers his salutations.

 HO DOES NOT KNOW, most sacred Majesty, that principal gifts are owed to princes, more principal gifts to great princes, and the most principal of all to the greatest? No one therefore will be puzzled that this little book is offered to you, on account of the excellence of the subject with which it is concerned, the originality of invention on which it depends, and the depth of demonstration whereby it is communicated, among the many other things that could be enumerated, since you are excellent in the sight of the people, most worthy by virtue of greatness of soul, most celebrated for the eminence of a sublime intellect, and indeed most distinguished, magnanimous, learned in all things, and indeed truly cultivated. It is yours to accept this graciously, to look on it with favor, and to examine it maturely and judiciously, that you will be seen as eminently generous, powerful, and wise.

FAREWELL.

✢

Merlin to the Artist

One who depicted the Gauls as cockerels,[4]
    Since he is not wholly imprudent,
    And hopes that his depiction is not found out
    As the inept work of an inept artist,
    Has appointed trusted servants and good friends,
    By whom he wishes more natural images to be driven far away.

Since you are not ignorant of this, you should worry
    When you present a true Gaul in more proper images
    Which cause all who have ears to marvel.
    Not being turned back by an importuning servant, you will repent.

---

4. A common bit of symbolism and also a Latin pun; *gallus* can mean either "Gaul, Frenchman" or "rooster."

Merlin to the Judges, on Sobriety

There is a river in Phrygia called Gallus.
  If you drink just a little of its water,
  It heals the ills of the body.

If you gulp it down like a drunkard, though,
  It will gulp you down entirely; you will die
  And never drink again.

In the same way, the writings of the wise,
  When scarcely touched, make life civilized
  And delightful in the highest degree.

Gorge yourself too much on them, though,
  And they will trouble you, or rather, drive you
  Headlong to madness or glory.

As you have so far been prudent, therefore,
  You have escaped such a punishment;
  In the judgment of the masters

It was enough to taste just so much wisdom
  As you may touch to your lips
  And sniff with your nostrils.

Thus I tell you that it is not well done
  When, now that you are a judge, you hurry so much
  That you shake your Midas ears.[5]

---

5. Midas, in Greek legend, was asked to judge a music contest between Apollo and the satyr
Marsyas, and judged that Marsyas was the better player. For this lapse of musical taste, Apollo
gave Midas donkey's ears, and Midas thus became the archetype of the inept critic.

Merlin to the Judges, on Appropriateness

That a dog has taken up plowing,
    That a camel wants to climb to the stars,
    That a shrew is hauled across the river by a frog,
    That those who ride a slow donkey hasten to arrive,
    That a cuckoo tries to catch wolves,
    Or pigs desire to fly:
    These are things poorly suited to nature.

But that fault is not found in this Organon of art;
    Nor in invitations to dig things up,
    Nor in fishing things out,
    Nor in flying through the air on one's own wings,
    Nor in teaching how to hunt and catch.

If you think yourselves proper diggers,
    And not unsuited to flying,
    Fishing, hunting, and catching,
    So that there will be no lamentations thereby,
    I will strike with you, striking together
    As you enter the labyrinth without a thread.

Preliminary Dialogue

An Apology for
On the Shadows of the Ideas
About the Author's Mnemonic Discovery

INTERLOCUTORS:
- HERMES
- PHILOTHIMUS
- LOGIFER

HERMES: Let's see what the book has to say. "You cannot be ignorant that the sun always remains the same, just this art remains the same. The same sun displays the acts of the honored and the deeds of the disgraced. When it rises, the sun brings grief to night-creatures such as the toad, the basilisk, and the owl, that are nocturnal, solitary, and consecrated to Pluto, while the rooster, phœnix, swan, eagle, lynx, ram, and lion greet it eagerly. When the sun rises, those who work in the shadows retreat to their lairs, while honest men and animals of light go forth to their work: the latter are called to labor, the former sent to rest.

"Lupine and heliotrope turn toward the sun, while the herbs and flowers of night turn away. The sun lifts up rarefacted moisture in the form of clouds, and casts it down condensed as rain to the earth. It gives to some things a perennial and continuing light, to others a changing light. The unwavering intellect teaches that the sun stands still, while the deceiving senses persuade us that it moves.[1] It rises when exposed to

---

1. A reference to the Copernican theory, of which Bruno was an early and vocal defender.

each place by the rotation of the earth, and sets at the same time to places otherwise disposed.

"By those whom we call 'Arctic dwellers,' on account of their difference of location, it seems to circle from left to right horizontally, but to many others it appears to traverse the heights and depths in an arc. It seems to have more of its circuit above the earth, and less below, because of its distance from us. In some portions of its semicircle it departs slowly, while in others it does so more quickly. In the south of the earth it seems to lean north, while in the north it appears to hasten south.

"Where the ground is flat, the sun's light is received in equal rays to either side, but in unequal rays where the ground slants. Between the two middle parallels of this great mass that perpetually inhabits space,[2] it perpetually bestows shadows of equal measure to the light, while doing this only in definite times elsewhere. The goddess Earth herself who nourishes us with her own back, so as to cast reproach in our faces, will obtain the sun's oblique rays for us, but reserves his direct rays for those she has placed atop her head.

"Certain moving bodies of the universe, which many understand to be living creatures and gods, following the leadership of One,[3] take the sun's light to themselves from their increase or (as it is called) their apogee, while others do the same in opposition or in middle latitudes, as they are called, and intervals. The moon, which other philosophers believe to be greater than the earth, turns one hemisphere toward all these same freely moving bodies, in order to receive their light, while to the earth she directs sorrowful shadows by the interposition of her globe, displaying the averse hemisphere of the moon.

"Therefore one and the same sun perpetually perseveres and remains, to one or another; disposed one way or another; accomplishing one thing or another. Not otherwise than the sun, we believe, will this art be, for one or another, to one or another."

PHILOTHIMUS: What are you saying to yourself, Hermes? What's the book you have in your hands?

---

2. The "mass" is the earth, the "middle parallels" the Tropics of Cancer and Capricorn.

3. These are the seven planets, believed to be living creatures and gods by the Greek Neoplatonist writers Bruno studied.

HERMES: The book is *On the Shadows of the Ideas*, about writing internally, and I'm of two minds about it. I'm not sure whether it ought to be published, or stay forever in the shadows where it has hidden for so long.

PHILOTHIMUS: Why is that?

HERMES: Because its author will be called conceited; as the saying goes, he lines up archers who aren't all equipped in the same way.

PHILOTHIMUS: If that really ought to be feared and avoided, no one would ever try to finish any truly worthwhile work, and nothing good and excellent would ever be published. The priests of Egypt said that the providence of the gods never stops sending some new Mercury to humanity at set intervals, even though they know he will get a bad reception from them, or none at all. The intellect never stops casting its illumination, nor does the visible sun, just because all of us don't always pay attention to them.

LOGIFER: I agree instead with those who think that a book like this certainly isn't publishable; I hear Philothimus voicing his doubts about that, but if he had heard what the two of us hear, Hermes, he would surely throw it onto the fire to be burned, rather than taking the trouble to see it in print. So far this sort of thing has not brought any happy result to those who study it, and so I don't know anything those who follow after them can hope for, except for a very little that they can understand all by themselves, as they would be able to figure out if they had the least bit of common sense.

PHILOTHIMUS: Do you hear what this fellow is saying?

HERMES: I do, and I would like to hear more. Discuss it between yourselves.

PHILOTHIMUS: Then I'll disagree with you, Logifer, and I should say this first: what you've said doesn't persuade, but rather, so to speak, stiffens the sinews of the opposite opinion. Those who aren't, with Hermes and myself, among the few who can reach an understanding of this art, shouldn't put forward their little praises, for those who haven't understood it aren't able to praise it or condemn it.

LOGIFER: You talk about what ought to be, not what will be, or is, or ever has been. Many of those who don't understand the art, precisely because they don't understand it, over and above the nastiness that drives their souls, heap up insults against the author and the art itself. Haven't you heard with your own ears Doctor Bobo,[4] who said there's no art of memory, only frequent efforts and regular repetition coupled together, so that what's seen many times is seen again, and what's heard many times is heard again?

PHILOTHIMUS: With a tail like that, he must be a monkey.

LOGIFER: How would you answer Master Anthoc,[5] who thinks that anyone who presents something beyond vulgar operations of memory, something greater or energized or different in some other way, is simply pretentious? You see how he's grown old in literary studies.

PHILOTHIMUS: I don't doubt for a moment that he's the nephew of that famous ass who was put in Noah's Ark to preserve the species.

LOGIFER: And there's Master Rocco,[6] the arch-master of arts and medicine, who prefers empirical doctrines of remembering, thinking that such trifles are better than the precepts of the artificial memory.

PHILOTHIMUS: Not outside of a pot.

LOGIFER: One of the old doctors said that none can succeed in this art unless their memory is naturally powerful.

PHILOTHIMUS: An opinion fallen off a bridge.

LOGIFER: Pharfacon, who's a doctor of both laws[7] and a learned philosopher, thinks that this art makes remembering harder rather than easier, since someone without the art just recalls the things themselves, but with the art we have to recall the things, the places, and a lot of images as well, and all this no doubt burdens and entangles the natural memory.

PHILOTHIMUS: He has the acumen of Crysippus, and his opinion ought to be inscribed on a big iron comb.

---

4. Bobo: Spanish, "idiot."

5. Anthoc: probably Greek ἀνθοκόμος, "flowery."

6. Rocco: Italian, "rock"; "blockhead" might be a good translation.

7. That is, of civil and church law.

LOGIFER: Doctor Berling[8] has said in his oration on the subject that not even the most learned can harvest anything useful from it, I believe, because he himself harvested nothing.

PHILOTHIMUS: What, are there no hedgehogs to be found under all these chestnuts?

LOGIFER: Master Maines[9] said, "Even if it pleases everyone else, it will never please me."

PHILOTHIMUS: He'd say the same thing about wine if he never tasted it.

LOGIFER: That famous fellow, your friend, what do you think his opinion would be?

PHILOTHIMUS: Put cuttlefish ink in a lamp and it makes white people look black; in the same way, a mind suffering from envy judges ugly things to be very clearly beautiful.

LOGIFER: It's said that the excellent Master Scoppet,[10] easily the first of physicians, in the middle of this tempest of ours, had this to say about our author: that he should have revealed his art of memory first to people he doesn't want to succeed, but isn't sure whether he wants them to fail because of scorn or incompetence.

PHILOTHIMUS: If he'd said "Show me your urine before displaying any more solid excrement," I don't doubt our author would have humored him, being truly very hospitable and civilized, and due to his dignity, his position, and his art, would have greeted him very agreeably.

LOGIFER: What should we say of Master Clyster,[11] the doctor of medicine whose final word it's improper to ignore? He differs not at all from what Arnaldo and Tiberius say, that it's better to give the tongue of a hoopoe to the forgetful, to grant a memory that holds tenaciously.

---

8. Berling: probably Italian *berlina*, "pillory."

9. Maines: probably French *mains*, "hands."

10. Scoppet: English, "shovel."

11. Clyster: Latin, "enema." The three names Maines, Scoppet and Clyster suggest a scatological joke about cures for constipation.

PHILOTHIMUS: Aristotle said that playing the lyre makes one a lyre-player. If someone were to put something on the head of the poor hoopoe who had its tongue pulled out, maybe by being doctored, it will turn into a doctor.

LOGIFER: Doctor Carpophorus[12] has also said, quoting Proculus and Sabinus, that the seats of mind and memory are triply distinct. Between the front and the back of the head, the pineal gland is the middle; when we work hard repeating something that is revealed by the memory, passage for the animal spirits opens up from the front to the back of the head. Now the animal spirits can only pass through something that is serene, lucid, and clear. When the brain is dulled on account of immoderate cold, it makes our memory sluggish and slow. If the cold combines with dryness, it brings excessive wakefulness and insomnia, while if it combines with moisture, the result is lethargy. To prevent these things, the medical art prescribes the following, to restore and excite the functioning of the mind, and rouse the spirit as though from base folly and lazy slumbers: moderation in sex; avoiding sorrow and drawing back from sensual pleasures; purging the body of all meats; massage of the head with an ivory comb and a rough cloth; drinking mild or watered wine, so as not to inflame the blood of the veins with strong wine; closing the pores of the stomach with things that are naturally or artificially styptic, so that fumes evaporating from the digestive process in the stomach don't obscure the mind and the intellect and lead to sleep; abstinence from cold and moist foods such as fish in general, brain, and marrow, as well as sharp and fume-producing foods such as leeks, radishes, onions, and capers, which are not digested well on account of their heat; using aromatic things; wiping the head and feet with a decoction of lemon balm, laurel, fennel, chamomile, iris, and the like; and Pythagorean exercises, done night and morning, as these most powerfully strengthen the memory, mind, and intellect. These are the things that comfort the memory, just as Democritus, Archigenes, Alexander, and Andronicus the Peripatetic handed down in their literary monuments, not these worthless arts that pretend to inflame the memory with I don't know what sort of images and figures.

PHILOTHIMUS: A strange lecture, finished off with a proper bellow; the venerable doctor leads forth parrots and asses.

---

12. Carpophorus: Greek καρποφόρος, "fruit-bearer."

LOGIFER: Master Arnophagus,[13] a particularly notable expert in justice and law, says that many learned people have no skill in this art, which they ought to have if it is all that you say.

PHILOTHIMUS: When a little girl hasn't yet cut her first teeth, we don't give her hard things to chew on.

LOGIFER: The art of Cicero, Thomas Aquinas, Albertus Magnus, Aludel, and other obscure authors appeared a long time ago, and none of those would be able to summon up the strength to challenge that most learned theologian and most subtle patriarch of literature, Master Psicoteus.[14]

PHILOTHIMUS: A judgment of the freshly tonsured.[15]

LOGIFER: And to sum it all up in a single word, various people think variously, diverse people speak diversely; there are as many opinions as there are heads.

PHILOTHIMUS: And as many voices. Crows caw, cuckoos call, wolves howl, pigs grunt, sheep bleat, cows moo, horses whinny, and asses bray. Aristotle said that it is ridiculous to ask any of those to respond to a question; cows moo to other cows, horses whinny to horses, asses bray to asses. This discussion of ours is aimed at persons of intelligence.

LOGIFER: True enough. Perhaps Hermes is willing to open the book, so that we can consider the author's own opinions.

HERMES: I'll do so gladly. This is from the preface to the work: "No one, I think, is unaware of the many arts of memory edited by others, every one of which are meant primarily for the use of church scholars who are versed in difficult matters. We have consulted these, so that we may set forth most of the fruits of their discoveries, of which the more important, useful, and easy material may indeed be considered necessary to treat of this illustrious and very desirable art. The older principles of training require prolonged exercise; they repel from their practice and study the lighter wits of the vulgar, who have less endurance and (if I

---

13. Arnophagus: Greek ἀρνοφάγος, "lamb eater."

14. Psicoteus: Greek ψιξόθεος, "god of crumbs." The "obscure authors" Logifer mentions were, of course, anything but obscure in Bruno's time.

15. That is, young novices in a monastery who had just received their first tonsure.

may say something very obvious) more impatience, the more subtle and ready to hand some work of genius is, and who think it is better to touch everything than grasp one thing firmly."

PHILOTHIMUS: To my mind, those who laugh at this author don't belong to the company of those who, collecting the opinions of others from here and there into a unity, for the sake of others' immortality, repay the labor expended by many authors for the sake of posterity. Rather, they belong to that much larger company who call themselves scholars, who haven't a bit of intelligence or reason, and so many times aren't able to achieve anything of the kind; who (having wrapped themselves up in a lion's skin they got one way or another from someone else) since they haven't produced anything, finally burst out talking when some feeble Mars among them (because it's easy to come up with inventions) gets spurted forth, or vomits up something from the poverty of a stupid mind. These? These are the battering rams of infants, the catapults of error, the bombards[16] of the inept, and the lightning flashes, thunder, and great tempests of the ignorant.

LOGIFER: Haven't you thought exactly the same thing of our songsters and poetasters, who try to market themselves to us as poets by strange inventions, half-verses and verses?

PHILOTHIMUS: Oh, let the poets alone. Just as kings' hands are supposed to have a long reach because of their rank, poets' voices are accustomed to reach just as far because of their profession and the times.

LOGIFER: I was talking about poetasters, not real poets.

PHILOTHIMUS: Well, few if any of them will think your dictum is meant for them. But what have they to do with our discussion? It's enough that in putting forth this art, the author is understood.

LOGIFER: Not by the poets.

PHILOTHIMUS: Granted, but let's return to the reading.

HERMES: He says: "Thus, having it in mind to oblige certain of my friends, I pursued other arts of memory of many kinds, which we each arranged diversely and in various ways, in order to communicate to each other the

---

16. Bombards: early cannons used in siege warfare.

value and applicability of each. In this way we have compiled this art out of the strengths of the more principal arts, containing the outstanding elements of all of them, and including nothing that ought to be left out. With this art I may certainly promise a method and knowledge that are easily practiced with little labor, while the meaning of the book itself is hardly accessible to all, as opposed to the custom of those whose books of this art are easy and quick, while their arts are difficult and lengthy to transmit. Few of these scholars understand this art, but any intelligent person may come and use it, and indeed all, whether ignorant or erudite, will easily be able to understand and practice it, and once they are well versed in it, they would be able to understand anything without a teacher, even in metaphysics and Platonic philosophy. For this art contains those; since it comprehends things by the exalted ends and preconceptions of the speculative faculty, it is able to comprehend anything that can be named (provided, however, that the mind using it is not stupid), but it still contains ends most proper to itself and most closely accommodated to things that are to be signified.

This art does not merely apply art to memory, but opens and introduces a way to the discovery of many different faculties. Therefore those who receive it should remember to hide it within themselves, since because of its dignity they should not casually spread it around. Scholars of the church, especially, are among those who ought to receive this, because of their abundant merits and capacities, and the more intense and patient training bestowed on them.

Beyond this, they will know in whose hands this art has fallen. We are not among those intellectuals who hold rigidly to some sort of strange philosophy, nor do we condemn others by means of some all-encompassing method of philosophizing. We do not fail to praise anyone who, using their own ingenuity to contemplate things, has devised some clever method. We do not abolish the Pythagorean mysteries; we do not belittle the Platonic faith; and we do not despise Peripatetic[17] reasoning, insofar as its foundations have really been established. We say this because we wish to lighten the troubles of those people who wish to use their own intellect to measure that of others; who are of that unfortunate kind who have long exercised themselves in the best philosophy, but not so far as to

---

17. Peripatetic: belonging to the school of Aristotle.

come up with their own opinions, and who in the final analysis lack any genius of their own and always rely on another's. These deserve more than those others who, ignorant of their own poverty, dare what should not be dared; the former should be tolerated, and even in a certain degree (unless they act out of negligence) ought to be praised. They are like those who are filled with the Aristotelian spirit, so that one expects to see improved books and speeches where these people have been heard or read.

On the Shadows of the Ideas! Such people will indeed be flabbergasted, saying that ideas are dreams or apparitions. If we should concede that, it will be asked if it is consistent with nature to say in any meaningful sense that one could run under the shadows of ideas? People might as well go rushing off toward the location of the rational soul. Giordano, they will say, you are talking about spinning or weaving the soul! Similarly, certain others will puff out their cheeks, drawing on the fruits of their self-discipline, in order to hold in a hostile comment, which I wish they would let out. We did the same thing when we understood less of the implications of the concept, when (which is the same thing) we took by faith what should have been grasped by knowedge. Now, with the benefit of better understanding, due to the acquisition and discovery of the ideas' own ultimate actions, we are able without contradiction to use the correct terms. Where Platonic terminology is convenient and its meanings are appropriate, it is accepted. Where Aristotelian meanings make for better expression in this art, though, they are faithfully admitted. Other schools are judged similarly.

Nor, indeed, have we invented one new term and tried to extend it to all things, for helmets, shields, swords, spears, banners, drums, horns, and other armaments of war are not produced and perfected in the same way. Furthermore, the discoveries of others who have attempted this work, not only those of Plato or Aristotle, will be useful in this project. In the same way, if the same people wonder why we appear to use customary terms, it is not because we desire them to mean something other than their usual meanings. Throughout this work, we make use of the diverse efforts of different philosophers, except where we introduce a better proposal of our own invention. Thus there is nothing here or in any of our other arts that should give people who are skilled in this kind of philosophizing any difficulty in understanding, provided that they pay attention.

We treat of this art under a twofold form and procedure. One is higher and applies more generally to all operations of the mind, and is the fount of many methods, out of which artificial memory may be grasped and discovered among many diverse instruments. It consists first of thirty intentions of the shadows, second of thirty conceptions of ideas, and thirdly of many combinations that can be made out of the intentions and concepts by industriously adapting the elements of the first wheel to the elements of those that follow. The other, which follows, focuses on a certain kind of comparative artificial memory.

Thirty Intentions of the Shadows

Intention I ✦ A[18]

ITH THE BLESSING of the one God, and the favor of the great gods who are under that highest prince,[19] we therefore begin.

The perfection of humanity, and the attainment of the best that can be had in this world, the wisest of the Hebrews introduces thus, speaking for his soul: "I sat under the shadow of Him whom I have desired."[20] Now it has been truly said that it is not in our nature to be able to dwell in the presence of truth. Human life is vanity. All is vanity, and that which is true and good is unique and first. That which is created so that, in itself, its being is not properly true, and its essence is not properly truth, can it have the efficacy and action of truth? To such a being it is sufficient, and more than sufficient, to sit under the shadow of goodness and truth. I do not say under the shadow of natural and rational goodness and truth, since this would necessarily imply falsehood and evil, but of metaphysical, ideal, and supersubstantial[21] goodness and truth. Thus the mind, participating in them by its own powers, is affected by goodness and truth; though it lacks so much of these that

---

18. Each of the thirty Intentions, like the thirty Concepts that follow, are labeled with a Latin, Greek, or Hebrew letter. These form a convenient shorthand for Bruno's philosophical algebra, and also a mnemonic tool; the images Bruno later assigns to these thirty letters allow words in Latin (or any Western language), Greek, and Hebrew to be memorized.

19. This fusion of monotheism and polytheism, though common in the Renaissance, cannot have endeared Bruno to the Church.

20. *Song of Solomon* 2:3.

21. Supersubstantial: A technical term in Renaissance philosophy, referring to the transcendent divine unity above substance, the highest level of reality.

it is but the image of these, it is nonetheless their image. The diaphane[22] of the soul, terminating in the opacity of the body itself, demands some image from which it may have a name, from the human mind, and the internal senses and reason that wraps us about while we live in the flesh. That image is the shadow.

Intention II ✣ B

When you have considered this, I desire that this next should occur to you: that you ought reasonably to draw a distinction between darkness and shadow. Shadow is not darkness; it is either the vestige of darkness in light, or the trace of light in darkness, or a participation of light and darkness, or a composite of light and darkness, or a mixture of light and darkness, or something in between light and darkness and distinct from both. This is either because shadow is not the full truth of light, or because it is false light, or because it is neither true nor false, but of those things that are a vestige of truth or falsehood, and so forth. But it may be taken as an axiom that shadow is the trace of light, or participation in light, but not full light.

Intention III ✣ C

Next you ought to remember that it is necessary to understand light in two aspects: one in the realm of substance,[23] the other in the realm of those things that are in relation to substance, or consist in substance (whence shadow also is understood according to a twofold opposition). The light that exists in relation to substance is the last vestige of the light that, they say, burst forth as the first act of Creation. The shadow that exists in relation to substance is in a like case compared with the shadow that, it is said, emanates from substance. That latter is itself called the first subject, and matter, by our natural philosophers.[24] None of those things that participate in it receive pure light; they are said, rather, to exist and act under the shadow of light.

---

22. Diaphane: The subtle body, of which the physical body is the densest layer.

23. Substance: A technical term in Renaissance philosophy, referring to pure formless matter, on which all qualities ("accidents") are impressed, like seals on wax. "Things that are in relation to substance" are the accidents.

24. "Natural philosophers" is a term used for alchemists in Bruno's time, and the "shadow that emanates from substance" is thus the mysterious First Matter of alchemy.

Intention IV ✢ D

Consequently, you should not pass over the fact that shadow possesses something of light, and something of darkness. A thing can come under shadow in two senses. That is, there is the shadow of darkness and, as they say, of death, when the powers of higher things dwindle and become idle, or subservient to lower things, when the soul in incarnation becomes so deeply turned toward the body and the senses. Then there is the shadow of light, when the powers of lower things, aspiring toward higher things, are made subject to eternal and more eminent objects so turned toward the heavens that the limitations of the flesh burden the spirit. In the former, the shadow inclines to darkness; in the latter, the shadow inclines to light. On the horizon of light and darkness, indeed, it is impossible to perceive anything but shadow, and likewise on the horizon of good and evil, or true and false. What can be made into good or evil, what can be falsified or formed according to truth, tending one way under one influence and another under another, is said to be shadow.

Intention V ✢ E

We ought specially to put forth for consideration those shadows that are the objects of desire and the cognitive faculty, conceived as a form of truth or goodness, which fall away into the realm of the senses from the supersubstantial unity by the increase of multitude, and proceed (to speak in the Pythagorean manner) to infinite multitude. To the extent that they recede from unity, they also depart from truth. This proceeds from that superessential[25] reality to essences, from essences to the things that are, and from those to their traces, images, simulacra, and shadows; then toward matter, to be hidden away in its recesses; and then finally toward the senses and the reason, so that they may be distinguished by these faculties.

---

25. In Bruno's sources, the divine unity is said to be superessential—beyond the essences of things—as well as supersubstantial—beyond the realm of matter. The following lines outline the descending levels of existence in Bruno's cosmos. "Essences" are the intelligences of the realm of absolute mind; the "things that are"—the term is borrowed from the *Poimandres*, the first treatise of the Corpus Hermeticum—are the stars and planets of the astral realm.

Intention VI ✛ F

Shadow in matter or nature, in natural things themselves, known by the internal or external senses, exists in a state of movement and alteration. Those things known by the intellect, and memory accords with the intellect, are at rest. Therefore the wise man[26] wrote about the natural and supersensual realms in the following manner: he causes the virgin to sit under the shadow of that desirable First, True, and Good. Since living according to nature, few persevere in that sitting or state of rest (because the senses leap on us at once and disturb us, and the phantasms that surround us, taking their lead from us, seduce us) that sitting is better denoted by verbs in the perfect or imperfect tense, rather than the present. Thus it says "I sat under the shadow," or "I was sitting."

Intention VII ✛ G

There is indeed order and connection in all things, so that lower bodies follow after middle, and middle after higher; composite things are unified by simple ones, and simple by even more simple; material things adhere to spiritual things, as do spiritual to material; so that of the universal being there might be one body, one order, one government, one principle, one end, one beginning, and one extreme. And since (as we have not disregarded Platonic principles) a continual outflowing proceeds from light to darkness, when something mental, turning toward matter and away from its proper action, submits to nature and fate, nothing hinders it from being called back from the depths step by step to the heights by the sound of Apollo's universal lyre,[27] and the lower, through intermediaries, submits to the nature of the higher. In the same way, in the realm of the senses, earth is rarefied into water, water into air, and air into fire, just as fire is condensed into air, air into water, and water into earth.

Thus in general we see that, in those things that undergo change, movement always ends in rest, and rest in movement. Likewise, that which always is and becomes in the heavens is considered best by the followers of Aristotle; since it may be said to have its proper act joined to its potential (whatever else may go into the proportions of this mixture), they hold that its end moves toward what comes before, and its beginning moves toward what follows. Thus, whatever may be decided about another kind of descent by the reasonings of theologians,

---

26. Solomon, in the passage from the *Song of Solomon* already cited.

27. Apollo's lyre: A standard Renaissance metaphor for the essential harmony uniting all things.

we resolutely intend that, by the excellent operations of the soul, always keeping the scale of nature[28] before our eyes, so that we may strive forward always from motion and multitude to stillness and unity through intrinsic operations, by virtue of that faculty in which we excel and through which we will also be shaped in many ways by wonderful divine operations. The visible link of things to this, and the consequences of that link, may comfort and encourage us.

The ancients knew and taught how human discourse might proceed from many individuals to one species,[29] ascending then from many species to one genus. They also knew and taught that the least intelligent understand each form as a distinct species; the less intelligent conceive all species distinctly by many different forms; the more intelligent by fewer forms, the most intelligent by one form, and that intelligence that is above all others by no form at all. Yet if the ancients knew how to perfect memory by proceeding from many species of things in memory, to one species that contains many things in memory, they certainly have not taught.

Intention VIII ✣ H

The nearest inferior is moved toward its nearest superior through certain intermediate steps by means of similarity. Certainly all these steps with their links exist, as they are indeed not similar, but the same, as those which will be described later. This, indeed, is how it happens that fire is fed with itself, while it does not attract water unless the water is assimilated to it in heat and rarefaction. By the connection of similarity, therefore, access is given from shadows to vestiges, vestiges to visible images, and visible images to other things.

Intention IX ✣ I

As each thing is indeed similar to its similars, it is equally similar to all its similars whether ascending, descending, or on the same level. So it happens that, within their limits, nature is able to make all things out of all things, and the intellect or reason is able to know all things from all things. Thus I say that as matter in all its forms takes form from all things, and the passive intellect (as it

---

28. Scale of nature: Literally "the ladder of nature," each rung of which is a level of being between divine unity and the world of sensory experience.

29. "Species" and "genus" are terms from medieval logic, used today only in biology and in the adjectives "specific" and "general." A species is a narrow class of entities (not necessarily living beings), composed of individuals; a genus is a broader type, composed of species.

is called) in all its forms is able to take form from all things, and memory can remember all things from all things; since every similar is made by its similar, every similar is known by its similar, and every similar is contained in its similar. Furthermore, a similar at a remote distance reaches toward its similar through the nearest intermediate similar.

Thus matter taken out of of a vegetable form does not take an animal form immediately, but is mediated through the form of chyle,[30] blood, and seed. Thus whoever knows the proper means between extremes can therefore, both naturally and rationally, draw all things out of all things.

Intention X ✢ K

Besides this, every similar passes to its similitudes through equality, and resonates with uniformity, or as it is called, equipotential. Proposing any other operation of the senses, whether internal or external senses are meant, would be useless and unhelpful. Thus it happens that what is similar to heat affects, not its similar, nor a lower level sharing in its similitude, but that which excells it, existing in a sensitive subject. Thus in practice you ought to bring back each memory image in the form in which you saw it earlier, so that, as you become skilled, they will not be prevented from entering your mind.

Intention XI ✢ L

Consider that if every part of this corporeal world were perfectly similar to every other, it would not be capable of beauty. The beauty of each part is likewise made manifest in the joining together of varied things, and in this same variety, the beauty of the whole consists. Thus the vision of a thing is a most imperfect vision, because the image displays variety, while the shadow that is cast by the figure extrinsically takes the form of many false definitions that exclude almost all variety. We may say this of the shadow insofar as it is shadow, but not insofar as we accept it as a proposition.

---

30. Chyle: In Renaissance medical theory, the nourishing fluid that results from digestion.

Intention XII ✢ M

The chaos of Anaxagoras[31] is indeed without ordered variety, and for this reason we contemplate the admirable order in the aforementioned variety of things. That order connects the higher to the lower and the lower to the higher, making that one great animal that is the world most beautiful by bringing all its parts into harmony. So much order requires an equal diversity, and so much diversity an equal order. For where there is no diversity, no order will be found to exist. Thus it is improper to think of the first principle[32] as ordered, or subject to order.

Intention XIII ✢ N

Since an indissoluble harmony connects the end of those things that are first with the beginnings of those that come after, and the feet of the foregoing with the heads of the following, you will be able to pull tight that golden chain[33] that extends from heaven to earth; you will be able to descend from heaven to earth, and ascend again to heaven in due order. By this grand and intricate connection we can lighten the burden of memory, since things that are remembered in an orderly fashion can be presented out of sequence, retaining the order within. This is shown in the following poem, where it is understood that Aries leads to Taurus, and its motion proceeds by diverse kinds of action to Gemini. From there by varied motions the action is carried in turn to Cancer, and similarly to the others in order, so that having grasped one intuitively, we can go on to the next at once, with no intermediate steps.

> Lord of the flock, he rushes forward, borne by
> His wrath and his paired feet, at the herd's monarch.
> The champion Bull, roused from vacant thoughts,
> Rushes impatiently to strike the Twins.
> The youths, closer than brothers, swiftly run
> To the waves. The Crab seeks greener pastures;
> Child of the waters, the Crab scuttles sidelong,

---

31. Anaxagoras: Greek philosopher, 500–428 BCE, who argued that the universe began from undifferentiated chaos.

32. First principle: Another term for the divine unity that forms the highest level of being.

33. This is the famous golden chain described in Homer's *Iliad*, used constantly in Renaissance writings as a metaphor for the Great Chain of Being connecting all things.

Boldly approaching the Lion's shaggy face.
Roused, the Lion runs upon long-haired limbs
Until the swift beast sights the straying Virgin.
He chases her; she flees; in a wild flight of footfalls
She runs to the man who wields the Balances.
While he is disturbed, as she clings to him passionately,
The curved sting of the Scorpion strikes him, wounding.
Fearing harm, he runs for the arts of medicine
Hoping to get behind the Archer,
Who, as though drunk, believing the Virgin is hurt,
Shoots an arrow at him but instead wounds the Goat.
Feeling deeply the first unfairly thrust iron,
the Goat flees into the rapidly falling waters;
Thus the wretched Goat is drawn into the watery abyss,
And trapped therein, this unusual food is given to the Fishes.

Intention XIV ✠ O

A certain ascent is made by connected and linked things toward the shadows of
the ideals. It is not made by a constant chain of similar links, first conceived in
the reasoning mind in words to be enunciated in order. Nor ought the links of
this chain be understood as the shadows beneath which Leviathan sleeps. This
is not shadow deprived of light, I say, but shadow conducing to light. Even if it
is not truth, it comes from truth and leads to truth, and so you should not think
of it as error, but as a veil of truth.

Intention XV ✠ P

You must therefore not confound what is signified by shadows with their hidden homonyms, so you do not fall into that kind of stupidity, that is, taking no
delight in shadows, you think, understand, and discern the opposition between
what is covered by other shadows (concerning which it is said, "shadows cover
the shadow of it") and what is raised above the level of bodies into the realm
of the intelligences. Concerning this it is said "His shadow overthrows moun-
tains." From this latter are drawn forth and emanated those things that produce
intelligence and memory in us, and in this the ascent toward the light reaches its
terminus. This or something similar was shown as a figure, as the Cabalists say,

by the veil that typically[34] or figuratively was said to be over the face of Moses, or rather figuratively, over the face of the Law. That was not for the purpose of deception, but so that it could be revealed to human eyes, which would be blinded if it were suddenly brought forth from darkness into light.

Nor, indeed, does nature endure a sudden movement from one extreme to the other; it is always mediated by shadows, and adumbrated by the light of the senses. The natural power of sight of some who pass from darkness to sudden light is so completely taken away that they may be put in the power of the thing they are examined. Shadow thus is a preparation for seeing the light. Shadow tempers the light. Through shadow, the divine form tempers and communicates information about things to the hungry eye and the soul dizzy with thirst. These shadows are therefore not extinguished by light, but preserve and care for the light that is in us. Remember that by them we are brought forward and led onward to intellect and memory.

Intention XVI ✣ Q

Of this the theologian[35] has said that unless you have believed, you will not understand; and philosophers have confirmed, in conceding and positing the things that faith is said to be (for faith, according to the Pythagoreans, belongs to the category of undemonstrated things; according to the Aristotelians, to that of undemonstrable things; and according to the Platonists, to both categories), that it is knowledge worth seeking, and among those things that contain something virtually, and radically, and by a certain implication, and ought to be pursued by us along a natural and rational course. Nature shows herself in veils before she reveals herself openly. It is likewise with God, and with the arts, which are dignified according to the divine and natural order. If difficulties are encountered in the practice of the shadows, therefore, and the suspicion arises that they are vain and do not give access to the light, this defect ought not to be attributed to the shadows. It is not enough to rearrange or cling to the coverings of things if you cannot grasp them in their nakedness.

---

34. Typically: That is, symbolically, according to the medieval theory of types, by which each incident in sacred writings could be read as the symbolic foreshadowing of some truth.

35. Tertullian, one of the first major Christian theologians.

Intention XVII ✠ R

The shadows we are discussing are contrary to physical shadows, such as those of trees and plants, which put serpents to flight and lull milder living things to sleep. Ideal shadows, if they are truly ideal, and bring all things back to the intellect and the purified inner sense, are different from these; they offer a way to rise up, and not a place beneath which to sleep.

Intention XVIII ✠ S

You will not sleep, either, if you proceed from inspecting physical shadows to the consideration of the corresponding ideal shadows. If a body moves away from our eyes and approaches a distant light, its shadow grows while it appears to become smaller; but if the same body recedes from the light, the shadow it casts becomes smaller, while the body itself becomes more of an impediment to our sight.

Intention XIX ✠ T

As the intensity of the light and the density of the body increase, the shadow given back from it becomes clearer, more prominent, and more definite, because in density and rarefaction, continuity and discontinuity, it imitates the body that casts it, and in fact the imitation may be detected by means of the body.

Intention XX ✠ V

The shadow follows the movement of the body and likewise of the light. Is the body moved? The shadow is moved. Is the light moved? The shadow is moved. Are body and light both moved? The shadow is moved. Contrary to the observations of physics, the same subject (that is, the subject that is moved) undergoes diverse and contrary movements at the same time.[36] What, then? Is it not necessary that the shadow follow the motion of the body with respect to the light, and also follow the motion of the light with respect to the body? Does this dissolve the necessity to move with both when they are moved at the same time to opposite sides? Moreover, notice how, when the light moves, the shadow moves as though fleeing from it, but when the body is moved, it moves as though following it. From this it may be seen that contrariety is not implied, but rather a concordance of opposites or contraries, in the flight of the

---

36. Aristotle's *Physics*, still the standard text in Bruno's time, rejects this as an impossibility.

one and the pursuit of the other. The two move differently in these cases, and proportionally in others. You ought to search and consider this for yourself, since we have already opened this matter far enough by these examples, which should guide your thoughts in these and other cases.

Intention XXI ✤ X

Let the similarity of the shadows to the ideas not escape your notice, for neither shadows nor ideas exist separately from their contraries. Things are recognized as beautiful or ugly, suitable or unsuitable, perfect or imperfect, and good or evil by reference to a single ideal form. Evil, imperfection, and ugliness, properly understood, do not belong to the ideas. Although they are called knowable rather than unknowable, and anything known by the intellect is known through the ideas, these things are known through an ideal form alien to them, not through their own proper form, which does not exist. What belongs to these things is not an existing existence (as I will explain more clearly later) but a deficient effect.[37]

Intention XXII ✤ Y

If you call a shadow an accident[38] of the body from which it is projected, you have an accident of one subject that goes away from it and returns to it, sometimes in the same form and sometimes only in the same number. If you want to call it an accident of the body onto which it is projected, then you make it an accident that can be separated from one subject so that it can wander over diverse subjects: if you move either the horse or the light, the shadow of the horse, formerly projected onto stone, is suddenly projected onto wood instead. This violates the theory of accidents in physics, unless you wish to plunge into Scylla by denying that shadows are accidents at all. What will we say then about the shadows of the ideas? You ought to be aware that these are neither substances nor accidents, but concepts that unite substances and accidents. If this is pleasing to your mind, and you decide to call them accidents of reason,

---

37. This is the classic Platonic argument that evil, imperfection, and ugliness are merely names for the insufficient manifestation of good, perfection, and beauty.

38. In Renaissance physics, an accident is a quality such as color or shape, imposed on substance like a seal on wax. According to the theory of accidents, an accident cannot exist apart from its substance—thus the accident "heavy" belongs to a stone, and does not flit from that stone to a nearby feather. Bruno argues here that this rule does not hold for shadows.

it should be said firmly that they are not habits, dispositions, or innate or accidental faculties;[39] the habits, dispositions, and faculties are produced by them and exist by them and through them. Rightly understood, then, substance and accident are not to be thought of as something universally distinct, as everyone has supposed until now. This distinction has not the least validity when reasoning about shadows.

Intention XXIII ✠ Z

A shadow is not subject to any time but its own time, any place but its own place, or any motion but its own motion. The same is true of its relationship to all pairs of opposites. In this way it is separated from all truth, but without truth it is not. Nor does it correspond ineptly to truth (if it be an ideal shadow) for it allows contrary and diverse things to be conceived as one. For nothing is contrary to shadow, which properly speaking is neither darkness nor light. To the shadow of the Tree of Knowledge, therefore, humanity resorts in order to understand darkness and light, true and false, good and evil, when God asks of him, ADAM, WHERE ART THOU?[40]

Intention XXIV ✠ Ψ (Psi)[41]

It must on no account be omitted from consideration that one opaque body placed opposite two or more lights projects two or more shadows. Understand from this in what way and by what means shadow follows a body, and in what way and by what means it follows light. Consider the way that many lights cast many shadows, and indeed innumerable lights cast innumerable shadows, even if these do not appear to the senses. Shadow here follows light in a different way, and may be seen to respond to light according to different principles.

Intention XXV ✠ Φ (Phi)

Nor should you pass over the fact that as a shadow flees light, it falsifies the measure of the body that casts it. Only at a certain unique distance, place and disposition is a shadow equal in length and breadth to the body produced

---

39. Habits, dispositions, and faculties were parts of mind in Renaissance theory.

40. *Genesis* 3:9.

41. The twenty-fourth through twenty-seventh intentions are symbolized by the Greek letters psi, phi, omega, and theta respectively. Since these letters have no Latin equivalents, they allow the user of Bruno's mnemonic methods to memorize Greek words.

opposite to the light, and in fact it will be found that such a shadow flees the light no further than the measure of the body casting the shadow. This is why the sun in certain places never makes shadows equal to the bodies that cast them, and in other places does so only rarely and for a short time.

Intention XXVI ✣ Ω (Omega)

If the size of the opaque body is greater than the size of the luminous body, it produces a cone of shadow with the narrow end in the opaque body and the base projected to infinity or limitless distance. But if the size of the light exceeds that of the opaque body, it produces a cone of shadow with the base in the opaque body and the point extending beyond the opaque body to a distance determined by the ratio by which the size of the luminous body is greater than the size of the opaque body. Hence the shadow that the luminous body of the moon would cast from the earth into the opposite part of the heavens (if the sun were absent from that hemisphere) has its narrow end determined by the margin of the earth, but its base, reaching almost to infinity beyond the earth, would not be determinable. But the shadow that the body of the sun casts from earth has the limits of the earth as a definite base, and its point does not touch the sphere of Mercury. You should judge similarly of the ideas and their shadows.

Intention XXVII ✣ Θ (Theta)

Note next how shadow is born from light and darkness (for I call the density of a body "darkness"), so that light is its father and darkness is its mother, and it does not exist unless both are present; and it follows light by fleeing from it, as though it were ashamed to be presented to its father by its mother on account of its form, so that out of shame it protests coming into its father's royal presence. It is like those who are so noble they cannot habitually parade about their own nobility, and so by their very modesty demonstrate it. Thus the shadow is attenuated as light increases, and is dilated as light contracts, and in this way it flees around the entire body.

Intention XXVIII ⚜ ע (Ayin)[42]

By putting a gnomon[43] perpendicularly above the ground between the north and the eye, and observing the shadow, we find the line of the meridian, and also infallibly measure intervals of time that are shown in order in the nightly circuit of the polar stars by the different parts of the circle of stars as they pass the line extended across their circumference. No less are the shadows of the ideals manifesting innumerable ideas by physical bodies able to signify to you the properties and differences of things.

Intention XXIX ⚜ צ (Tzaddi)

The sun casts six different cardinal shadows. One goes to the east, the shadow of a body cast as the sun is setting. One goes to the west, extending away from the sun as it rises. One is cast at noon, when the sun is in southern latitudes, toward the north. One is cast when the sun is in northern latitudes, toward the south.[44] One is cast when the sun is directly overhead; from the zone (as it is called) of heaven, rays extend perpendicularly toward the nadir, casting the shadow of the earth. From the other side of the sky, however, is cast an attenuated shadow upwards. It is thus for us in the horizon of nature, on the same equally balanced and perfect sphere, under the equinox of the senses or the equidies[45] of the intellect. Under the eternal ideas are constituted six kinds of shadows that, we are able to understand, all can be converted into light.

Intention XXX ⚜ ש (Shin)

So you should understand well that all kinds of shadows may be ultimately referred to the six cardinal shadows. No less ought you to know that all shadows

---

42. The twenty-eighth through thirtieth intentions are symbolized by the Hebrew letters ayin, tzaddi, and shin respectively. These have no equivalents in either the Latin or Greek alphabets, allowing the user of Bruno's methods to memorize Hebrew words.

43. Gnomon: The vertical part of a sundial, or a pole used to cast shadows.

44. That is, in the southern hemisphere, the sun is in the northern sky and casts shadows southward at noon; in the northern hemisphere the sun is in the southern sky and casts shadows northward at noon.

45. This is an astronomical pun; *equinox* literally means "equal night," and Bruno contrasts the metaphoric darkness of the "night of the senses" with the *equidies* or "equal day" of the luminous intellect.

ought ultimately to be reduced to one source most fecund and another most general.[46] In our proposition, I assert, one shadow can be the shadow of all ideas, producing, judging, and prefiguring all other things by addition, subtraction, and generally speaking by alteration.[47] It is the same in art, where all things take into themselves alterations, transpositions, and diversifications universally, through the substantial subject in terms of matter, but through the adject in terms of form.[48] All these admit certain analogies with metaphysics, logic, and physics, or with preternatural, natural, and rational things. Image and shadow are just the same. In the divine mind, each idea is unique but united with all. In the realm of intelligences they are ideas with separate manifestations. In the heavens, they are potentials acting multiply and successively. In nature, they take the form of traces, like impressions in wax. In the human will and reason, they take the form of shadows.[49]

Here is a diagram [Figure 2] of the way that one idea contains an infinite difference of things in expression, and one shadow an infinite difference in potential. From horizontal line AB extend the vertical line CD perpendicularly, creating two right angles. If the vertical line then inclines toward B, it would produce an acute angle

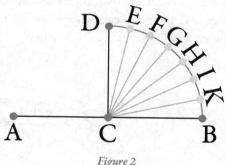

Figure 2

on one side and an obtuse angle on the other. As it inclines more and more, to F, G, H, I, K, and so on in order, the angles become respectively more acute and obtuse. In this way is shown how these two straight lines contain the potential

---

46. That is, solid matter (the "most fecund" source) and light (the "most general").

47. This passage closely echoes the Emerald Tablet of Hermes: "And as all things were from one, by the mediation of one, so from this one thing come all things by adaptation."

48. "Substantial subject" is a technical term for pure unformed matter, "adject" for the accidents impressed on matter. Both subject and adject appear later in the book as different types of memory images.

49. Here again Bruno outlines the cosmos of Renaissance magic in descending order: the divine unity above all; the empyrean realm of pure intelligences; the astral or celestial realm; the realm of material nature; and the realm of the human mind.

for an infinite number of different acute and obtuse angles. In the First Cause[50] this potential is not different from its expression, for in it, whatever is able to be, is; to be and to be able are identical in it. This is why, in the diagram, D remains one and the same despite an infinite difference of angles. In the power that drives the heavens,[51] the potential is active, like a hand that makes the line move to points E, F, G, and innumerable others, but does not move itself. In the heavens it is a mixture of active and passive, like line CD, which can be moved to make one angle or another. In the same way, the heavenly ideas are said by the Peripatetics to have the expression of their potential in mixture. In those things moved by the heavens and in matter, the potential is passive, signified by D, whose power is revealed through innumerable differences of acute and obtuse angles, through modes of being in matter and effect, and by participating in action. What we have said about angles may be applied just as well to any difference in kind that can be expressed by numbers. In this way anything can be shown clearly using anything you like.

✣

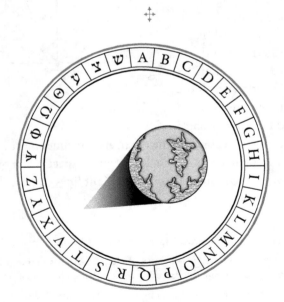

*Figure 3. **Figure of Shadows***

---

50. Another term for the divine unity.

51. Another way of talking about the empyrean, the realm of intelligences.

Thirty Conceptions of the Ideas

 EXT WE PROCEED to the thirty conceptions of the Ideas, first by themselves and then conceived together with the intentions of the shadows.

Conception I ⁜ A

God, according to Plotinus, fashioned eyes in the face to receive the light, and applied instruments to the other senses, that they should at times naturally serve the light, and at other times limit what can be known by the light.[52] Doubtless by these words he revealed some special thing pertaining to the things of the intelligible world.

Conception II ⁜ B

It is inappropriate to think of this world of ours as having several rulers, and thus of having more than one order. Consequently, if the world has one order, each of its members is joined and subordinated to other members. Thus higher things, insofar as they more truly exist, reach out toward matter, extending themselves in mass and multiplying themselves in number, proceeding from what most fully exists in itself, to what has the least existence, and cannot even be said to exist in its own right. This order has its steps, which may be conceived mentally, drawing an image of the great world from the world that naturally exists within oneself. By this means, acting as though through nature, it acts without hindrance throughout the universe.[53]

---

52. In section 1 of Ennead VI.7, "On the Multiplicity of the Ideas."
53. This is the fundamental thesis of Renaissance magic.

Conception III ✣ C

Concerning those things that are always the same, there is room for neither discussion nor argument. If anything had been shown always to be the same, the point of arguing about it or discussing it would be taken away. But such a thing completes its own work, so that a certain external image of itself is unfolded and produced out of itself, as though by nature. By this process, as it proceeds repeatedly and frequently, the image approaches nearer to its similitude. As thought and awareness become less and less involved, the more perfectly and exquisitely the process goes. This process therefore exists in space and time, while the patterns of the ideas are free of space and time, being conformed to divine beings in their activities, or pertaining to intellect or will. This is likely what was meant by the writer[54] who said, "We exist in the flesh but we do not live according to the flesh."

Conception IV ✣ D

This is possible and true, if the intellectual soul is in no sense grafted onto or fixed into the body, and ought not to be understood as existing in the body, but simply assisting and governing the body,[55] so that its form is able to approach perfection only when it is separated from the body. This opinion the famous Theologian[56] indisputably agreed with most completely, and gave that more perfect being a name, calling it the "inner man." If you wish to confirm this, and ask what operations are possible without the body, consider how ideas are brought together, free of the restrictions of space and time, whenever a human being, freed by mind or soul, abandons matter and time.

Conception V ✣ E

The soul possesses substance,[57] and the highest intellect is to its own substance, as a diaphanous body is to light, as the leading Platonists have understood. The

---

54. St. Augustine.

55. That is, the soul is not an accident of the body, and can exist apart from it. The similarity to Bruno's theory of shadows is not accidental.

56. Thomas Aquinas.

57. Another reference to Bruno's view that the soul is not an accident of the body; it is not possessed by substance, but rather it possesses the substance of the body.

body's diaphanity and transparency admits some of the soul's innate luminosity, which is always active when it is apart from the body and, so to speak, inhabits a region of light. But living in the body, it is as though its crystalline diaphanity terminates in opacity; it takes the wandering forms of sensible things, which approach it and recede from it as it turns toward and away from them, according to different times and places.

Conception VI ✝ F

The forms of things are in the ideas; in a certain way, they are in themselves; they are in heaven; they are in the cycles of heaven; they are in proximate seminal causes; they are in proximate efficient causes; they are individually present in their effects; they are in light; they are in the senses, both intrinsically and extrinsically; each in its own way.

Conception VII ✝ G

Matter is not filled up by receiving forms. It is eternally affected by new forms without complaining, because it neither truly accepts nor truly receives what it appears to receive. For the things that truly are, are not themselves sensible or individual; rather, I assert that they may first, principally, and most be termed substances. For the things that truly are, always remain; those things that are subject to generation and corruption are not truly called substances. This distinction is not only pleasing to those who philosophize rightly, but we have also heard theologians describing the outer man under this natural condition as vanity. Everything else that comes into being under the sun, that is, everything that exists in the material region of the universe, they also put under the heading of vanity. From the ideas, and from the ideas alone, the soul seeks fixed conceptions, if you understand.

Conception VIII ✢ H

The idea is the first man.[58] The soul is the second. The third is almost not human at all, said Plotinus, where he explains the reason why there are many ideas.[59] The second depends on the first, and the third from the second, during the time that by ordination, contraction, and composition, the man is ordained to physical existence. Conceived metaphysically, therefore, the third ascends into the second, and the second into the first.

Conception IX ✢ I

The unchanging, the abiding, and the eternal coincide. What is unchanging, because it is unchanging, abides and is eternal. What is eternal, because it is eternal, abides and does not change. The abiding, because it abides, is unchanging and eternal. You ought therefore to strive for the unchanging, or that which has the principle of its identity in itself, that you may have it permanently and persistently. If you take this, you will have a beginning from which you may make fixed species in your soul.

Conception X ✢ K

This teaching is so valuable that it should be fixed in the mind. Intellect is the first light of Amphitrite;[60] thus she pours forth her light from her innermost recesses to external things, and draws things inward from the extremes, so that by this capacity, anything you wish may be drawn out from itself and joined to all things, and by this faculty anything you like may reach out along the path of the same light. This, indeed, is what one meant in saying, JOIN THE END TO THE BEGINNING, and another in saying, THERE IS NONE WHO CAN ESCAPE HIS WRATH. I understand by the first, the intelligible light that extends from God and to Him, and by the other, the intelligibility that accompanies this. As

---

58. This refers to the Platonic principle that the idea or immortal principle, also called the spirit, is the first or primary part of a human being; the soul or vital principle is secondary, while the body is animal rather than truly human.

59. In sections 4-6 of Ennead VI.7, "On the Multiplicity of the Ideas."

60. In Greek mythology Amphitrite was the wife of Poseidon, god of the sea; Pythagorean symbolism assigned her to the number 6. The intellect corresponds to Athena and the number 7, the first number that proceeds from 6.

it flows from one thing to another, and from diverse things to others as diverse, it is multiplied beyond numbering, so that only those who can count the multitude of stars can count them; and yet it flows back and is rejoined to the same unity that is the fount of all unity.

Conception XI ✢ L

The first intellect in its fecundity sends forth ideas in its own way, but the ideas are not new, nor are they sent forth in a new way. Nature produces numerous new things, but she does not produce them each in its own new way, since she always works according to the same way. Reason forms new things in new ways, and in infinite species: composing, dividing, abstracting, combining, adding, subtracting, ordering, and disordering.

Conception XII ✢ M

Animals of hideous shape are beautiful in heaven. Metals that do not shine in themselves shine in their planets.[61] Neither humanity, nor animals, nor metals exist here as they do in heaven. What runs about randomly here, flourishes in its proper action there, through the movements of higher powers. Virtues that here unfold toward matter, there are united and infolded toward their essential act. From this is made clear the Platonist saying that the idea of anything, even an inanimate thing, is something alive and intelligent. Likewise, in the first mind, the idea of all things is one. Therefore it is by illuminating, vivifying, and unifying that you are conformed to the higher powers, and exalted in conceiving and retaining images.

Conception XIII ✢ N

It contains light, the life of intelligence, and the first unity, as well as all forms, perfections, truths, numbers, and the scale of things.[62] What in nature are different, contrary, and diverse, in it are identical, harmonious, and one. See, then, if you can bring all species to identity, concord, and unity by your own powers,

---

61. In Renaissance theory, every metal—not merely the seven traditional planetary metals—corresponds to one of the planets.

62. "It" here is the divine unity or first mind.

without wearying your imagination, disturbing your mind, or confounding your memory.

Conception XIV ✢ O

You should begin with the intention to conform physical bodies to the visible heavens, so that the forms of lesser animals, even the basest, may in a proportion that is far from base rest on unfleeting feet, but strive further toward conformity with the intellectual heaven, which possesses all the forms of the world in a way that surpasses the visible heavens.[63]

Conception XV ✢ P

Just such a progress you will next learn to make, and you will experience the passage from a confused multiplicity to a distinct unity as you proceed. This is not a matter of melting down all distinctions through a universal logic that pursues its way from distinct lower species, through middle species that are confused, to supreme species that are even more confused. Rather, it passes from unformed and multiple parts, and fits them to itself, formed, whole, and one. When the hand is joined to the arm, the foot to the leg, and the eye to the face, they may be known more fully in their combination than when situated apart. It is the same with the parts and species of the universe; nothing should be studied by itself and exempted from the universal order, which is absolutely simple, perfect, and prior to number in the first mind. If we recognize that each thing must be connected to all others, and unified by proportion, what is there that we may not understand, remember, and accomplish?

Conception XVI ✢ Q

Unity is that which defines all things. Unity is the splendor of beauty in all things. One lightning flashes forth from the multitude of species. If you would make the attempt, place that before your eyes, and see all interposing visible things in a universal way, so that nothing at all may escape you.

---

63. This passage critiques the teachings of Marsilio Ficino, whose *De Vita Cœlitus Comparanda* urged the use of planetary magic to harmonize the human body with the heavens; Bruno argues that this is a preliminary stage to harmonizing the whole self with the realm of ideas through his own magical mnemonic art.

Conception XVII ✟ R

Error and oblivion fall to our lot, since among human beings, weaknesses sprout from our form and composition. Because of the formation of the corporeal world, its form is inferior, since it is composed of traces and deformities. Therefore you should ascend to the realm where species are pure, nothing is formless, and all is formed according to the same form.

Conception XVIII ✟ S

Plotinus, the prince of Platonists, taught that as long as the eyes gaze outward to admire some manifested figure, the soul is not yet seized by love. Only when the soul first returns to itself from externals, does it conceive in itself figures that are unmanifest and transcending sight, and then love dawns forthwith. This is as true of intelligible objects as it is of desirable ones. From this, therefore, you may investigate how species are conceived more quickly, lively, and tenaciously.

Conception XIX ✟ T

Plotinus recognized seven steps, to which we add two more, forming a ladder that ascends to the first realities. The first of these is the purification of the soul. The second is attention. The third is intention. The fourth is contemplation of order. The fifth is proportional analogy drawn from order. The sixth is negation or separation. The seventh is sacrifice. The eighth is the transformation of the self into its goal. The ninth is the transformation of the goal into itself. Thus an opening, an access, and an entrance will be made from the shadows to the ideas.

Conception XX ✟ V

All that is, after unity, is necessarily multiplex and numerous. Other than the one and first, therefore, all things are numbered. Thus beneath the lowest step of the scale of nature is infinite number, or matter. In the highest, by contrast, is infinite unity and pure act. Therefore descent, dispersion, and uncertaintly go toward matter. Ascent, concentration, and determination go toward act.

Conception XXI ✟ X

By numbers, according to some, beings take to themselves what truly is, that is, true being, just as matter through inchoate forms takes to itself form.

Conception XXII ✣ Y

You should consider form in three aspects. The first is that from which a thing itself comes to be formed, so that it is able to accomplish its act; we properly do not call this first aspect an idea, but simply things that produce form. The second is that by which a thing is formed, as though part of the thing; and this may not be called similar to an idea, since it is simply a part. The third is that which defines a thing and shapes it as an inherent quality; this cannot be described as an idea, since their form cannot be separated from the thing. The fourth is that according to which something is formed, and which something imitates, and in common parlance this customarily has the name of idea. It is said to exist in four ways: in the crafts, before the products of craft; in first principles, before the second; in the laws of nature, before natural things; and in the divine mind, before nature and the universe. The first is called technical, the second logical, the third physical, and the fourth metaphysical.

Conception XXIII ✣ Z

Certain forms are imitated from nature, the way images in a mirror reflect the forms of things. Others are imitated from culture, the way the pattern of a seal is impressed in wax. According to another classification, some are imitated as though by themselves, like a painting that depicts something by the painter's intention. Some are half by accident and half by themselves, like a painting made to depict what it has to depict. Some are by sheer happenstance, as when something happens to look like something without any intention causing it. Some, finally, are neither by themselves nor by accident; they depict nothing beyond themselves, nor is it possible to refer an imitation to them, if such things can really be called forms. In the first class, idea has a large part; in the second, a small part; in the third, the least part; and in the fourth, no part at all.

Conception XXIV ✣ Ψ

Action that comes from nature and from chance, and not from a deliberate act of will, is not subject to ideas. If such were the first cause, there would be no ideas, and action would not be the result of choice. Democritus, Empedocles, and Epicurus[64] thought otherwise. If you hold that it is impossible for the prin-

---

64. Greek philosophers who argued that material atoms were the first principle of all things.

ciple of action to be separated from anything, and thus rendered unsuitable to all, unless all possible things be returned to it, many things will be returned to it.

Conception XXV ✢ Φ

Unity is called innate in us. The form of an exemplar holds to the limit of proportion, and by its act it accepts the active form because the exemplar is beyond it. It is not, however, proper to think that God obeys ends outside himself, and accepts from another source that it is sufficient for him to act. This is why ideas do not exist outside Him. For our part, though, we ought to seek them outside and above us, as within us we have only their shadows.

Conception XXVI ✢ Ω

By the species that are in intellect, a thing may be apprehended better than by the species that are in physical subjects, which are more deeply immersed in matter. Similarly, a thing may be better understood by species of things that are in the divine mind, than by those that exist in their own right. Two things are required for a species to be a medium of understanding: first, a representation of the thing to be known that is suitable by its propinquity to the understanding and spiritual being, and second a representation in matter of that which has its existence in the understanding.

Conception XXVII ✢ Θ

Ideas are the principal forms of things, according to which all things that arise and pass away are formed, and they refer not only to what is generated and corrupted, but also to everything that is able to be generated and pass away. Following thereafter, we form in ourselves shadows of ideas, when such allow enough facility and tractability that they may be adapted to all possible formations. We have made a certain similitude of this process, consisting of a set of turning wheels. Still, if another approach tempts you, attempt it.

Conception XXVIII ✢ ℣

Plato did not posit ideas of accidents. In fact, he understood the ideas to be the proximate causes of things, and if something other than ideas had been the proximate cause of things, then he would not have accepted the existence of ideas, and therefore accepted what by earlier and later writers was said not to be a common idea, but a first existence followed by the ideas. This is why the philosopher Clement[65] held that ideas were inferior to the highest existences.

Theologians, by contrast, hold that there are ideas of accidents, because they understand God to be the immediate cause of all things, without excluding secondary gods or causes. That is why we hold here that there are ideas of all things, because we rise up to ideas from every conceivable thing. From everything, indeed, we form ideal shadows. Nor do we cast down the Platonic doctrine; rather, we open them to the intelligent.

Conception XXIX ✤ ﬩

Plato did not posit ideas of individual things, but only of species, because ideas pertain to the production of forms alone, not to material existences, and also because forms, rather than genera or individuals, are principally intended by nature.

Theologians, by contrast, posit that there are ideas of individuals, because they assert that the total cause of both matter and form is God. We likewise hold that there are forms of individuals, because we fashion our idea-making principles according to universal patterns and the apprehension of similitudes: whether prior to the thing, in the thing, the thing itself, or after the thing; and likewise whether in sense or intellect, and in practice or theory.

Conception XXX ✤ ﬩

Ideas of a less general kind have their source in more general ideas, and ultimately the genera of all ideas unite in that first existence, which is called the highest intelligible. In the same way you ought to establish less general shadows of ideas in the more general, and the less common extrinsic subjects in the more common.

---

65. Clement of Alexandria, a Christian Neoplatonist of the late 2nd and early 3rd centuries.

Figure 4. *Figure of the Intention of the Ideas*

On Combining
the First Wheel with the Second

It will be found best to direct the will through the same general art by a combination of intellect, will, and memory, provided that we bring all their perceptions together when presenting it to the memory. First, learn the primary elements with their significations. Next, the secondary. Third, the secondary elements deduced from the primary. The first two we have shown here, so that by the turning of the wheel you will be led through the doctrines of the Peripatetics and Platonists. The third we leave to your own industry.

Next, drawing together these universal intentions, we proceed to take up their application to the art of memory.

The Art of Memory
of Giordano Bruno

I

E CONSIDER THIS ART to belong to the shadows of the ideas, since it rouses the sluggish nature that already exists, or it directs and guides the wayward and exorbitant, or it strengthens and sustains the weak and weary, or it corrects the erring, or it follows the perfect and emulates the industrious.

II

It is indeed the sort of thing that ought to be put in the category of the architecture of discourse,[66] and it follows a certain habit of reasoning in the mind, which proceeds from the life principle of the world to the life principle of each individual thing that comes forth, and of all individual things together. Nothing depends on that power as though hanging from a branch, nor by some peculiar faculty emerging from it. Rather, all share the same trunk, since the same essence of the universal soul indwells all. I think that the same principle applies here:[67] if the art consisted in the power of memory, how would it issue from the intellect? And if it consisted in the power of intellect, how would it proceed out of memory, sensation, and desire? Rather, through one and the same thing we

---

66. The art of memory was traditionally one of the disciplines belonging to rhetoric.

67. That is, just as one soul (the *anima mundi* or world-soul) indwells all things in the world, so one art—the secret art of Bruno's *Clavis Magna*—includes both the art of memory and the art of reasoning.

are regulated and directed toward what is to be understood, discussed, memorized, imagined, desired, and whatever we wish to be perceived.

III

But it is not enough to begin by asking what carries the mind generally to each and all of its functions. It is necessary also to ask by what means the mind acquires an art. By what art does the mind acquire an art? Is it not proper to call "art" what nature, the mother of skill, strives to master through frequent repetitions?

IV

Would it not be proper to say that before all other arts there exists one art that we may call "organic," as it works through many organons: an art that is not itself an organon,[68] but functions through organons? Is it not proper to call something an art when it makes the instruments of art? What would it be, if not an art? Since the organon that creates other organons takes precedence over them, expound to me the reason why another art ought to precede this art. Wherein does an organic art excel, that agents[69] are subject to it? In all doubts proceeding from the nature of that which comes before it. Those, in a certain sense, have been made susceptible to diminution in the innermost recesses of the primary organon. While common philosophers are apt to name the essence from the external form of things, we demur, as it is customary to put reasoning methods in the category of extrinsic form, as though art is not to be found in the innermost recesses of matter. But this is far from our intention and should not be interpreted as such.

V

The case is rather as it appears to the better philosophers: of that which is first, nothing else can be said; as the natural faculties are born together with reason, with the seeds of primal principles, the potentials within which are drawn by

---

68. An organon, in Greek as well as philosopher's English, means an instrument, tool, or organ, and has the additional meaning (from its use by Aristotle) of a comprehensive method for thinking; Bruno means all four of these, so I have used his word here.

69. An agent is anything that acts on something else; a patient is anything that is acted on.

extrinsic objects as though by a lure, and by the intellectual agents as though by the sun's light; and by the eternal Ideas as though they received the influences of the stars flowing together through a medium; as it is ordained by the best and highest of all, which fecundates all in action, so that each proceeds to its proper end by means of its own powers. It is manifest from this that when we wish to call this art the natural fount of all arts, we do not do so rashly.

VI

It is with a considered intention, therefore, that we can say that in some things art exceeds nature, and in others it is surpassed by her. The former is less possible with the more remote acts of nature, but may be said with more reason of those things nearer to us that we are able to examine. A thing can perpetuate the substantial form of something in the same species, which cannot perpetuate it in the same number, for in this art the faculties are not extended. Thus the extrinsic form and figure is the revealer of the great key; by art it is committed to hard stone or diamond. Likewise, the conditions, acts, and name of memory, and the objects of understanding that are to be perpetuated, are committed, which nature would not have been able to retain; since the stomach of changeable matter promptly digests all things.

VII

Whence, I ask, come the faculties of this art? Beyond a doubt, from the source whence genius springs. Next, the genius of what? Of man. And man, with all his faculties, whence comes he? Surely, he is born of nature. If you would contemplate the thing from the beginning, therefore, and wish to dig up this tree by the roots in order to transplant it, it is inclined by nature to cultivation and recognition. You will surely excel in it who, shouting and clamoring in the beginning, direct your soul toward the fearful things that we illuminate. Nature is what confines the soul in the body; nature furnishes fitting instruments to the soul. (It is from this that the Pythagoreans, and the wisest of the magicians, claimed to perceive the shape of the life and soul in the form of the body.[70]) Nature herself submits to you in all things (unless you turn away from her). Universal

---

70. The art of physiognomy, or reading the personality and destiny of an individual from the shape of his or her body, was common in Bruno's time.

nature is not composed in such a way as to fail in her duty to us, for Jupiter rains upon all shoots, and over all plants benign Apollo rises. Still, not all things are endowed equally with life by the things above them; though all things equally turn toward the higher, so that it may be clearly seen in us what by our own selves is separated from that communion.

VIII

Thus nature stands above everything possible, whether before natural things, or in natural things, or through natural things. You should therefore understand that every action begins with nature, and you should not forget to guide nature by itself. You may distinguish this however you like from the positive agent in the vulgar natural philosophy; I do not teach this. Still, I would admit under oath that just as that is distinguished, so the organ that operates is distinguished from that which is operated on, as the medium from the source, and the arm from that which it shakes.

IX

You should therefore understand that we are not following the vulgar philosophy, in which the name of nature is applied to matter and form, but rather that we recognize the intrinsic principle of nature; whether it be common to all, or supposed in this case, or has been contracted to it. Thus we gladly listen to the speeches of idiots when they compare the nature of that person with the nature of this one; not because it is possible to apprehend nature according to universal logic, or according to similitudes, but rather according to the physical, which sometimes is in all things, and at other times is contracted to individual things.

X

Thus things that are past and absent can represent things that are present and visible; thence we can perceive sensible things by sculptures and pictures. In the same way, transient words brought forth in empty air, may be made enduring by writing. In this way conceptions that are expressed, just like those that are silent, become communicable, and are transmitted to all places and times.

XI

What commonly is called either fate, or necessity, or the Good, or Demogorgon,[71] or the *anima mundi*,[72] or nature, is communicated to the things below it, drawing them from imperfection to perfection; it proceeds in motion and time, being the beginning of these in the whole and in each thing. The arts are said to progress in the same manner, as though by a guiding hand.

Thus (and this points toward the proposition we have in mind) it is said that the ancients once wrote with knives on tree bark. In a succeeding age, they wrote with a stylus on stones they dug from the ground; this was followed by papyrus written upon with ink from squids. Then came parchment with ink darkened artificially, and thereafter paper and water-based inks were brought into use, and proved to be far more apt for writing. The art of writing thus progressed from knives to styluses, from styluses to sponges, from sponges to reeds, from reeds to pens, and from pens, finally, to cast type.

In the same manner as may be seen in the development of writing, we judge internal writing to have proceeded; from the beginning of humane studies, whether it had its origin with Simonides of Melos[73] or from some other; which put places and images in place of paper and letters, and imaginative and cogitative acts in place of the scribe and his reed pen; thus they learned to inscribe the species of the things that were to be memorized in an internal book. With what diligence, and what and how much we have been able to add, and how much we have been able to draw together from these monuments, you may be the judge. Those that we have made have all been added as a result of practice.

XII

In the book *The Great Key*[74] you will find twelve subjects presented: species, forms, simulacra, images, apparitions, examples, traces, indices, signs, notes, characters, and sigils.[75] Some of these refer to things perceptible by the eyes (or,

---

71. Demogorgon: the god or ruler of the elves and fays in Renaissance literary culture.

72. *Anima mundi*: the soul of the world, a central concept in Renaissance occult philosophy.

73. The traditional founder of the art of memory in ancient Greece.

74. Bruno's unpublished book, in which he expounds his system in its entirety.

75. These are technical terms in Renaissance philosophy. The last three in particular were specifically magical terms, and are defined in the Glossary.

in figurative language, things created by nature rather than art); these include external form, image, or example, which by painting, or some other figurative art that emulates its mother,[76] describes many things, and are described by them.

Some are referred to the internal sense, in which they are magnified, distributed, and multiplied in measure, duration, and number; so that, having been drawn together into phantasms, they offer themselves to that faculty.

There are some that turn one way and another on the same point of similitude; for example, they make an example using a form of the same genus and a substance of the same species. Some lack their own proper substance, so that it is perfectly clear in what way the sophist lies about reality; as art imitates nature universally. Some, indeed, are assigned to art, in such a way that they are seen to be approved by nature; these are signs, notes, characters, and sigils, in which there is so much power that they may be seen to act beyond nature, above nature, and if circumstances require it, against nature.

XIII

These latter may be used whenever figures and images are unable to do what is required; that is, when what is to be memorized does not remain in the genus of things that can be imagined or figured. These lack those accidents by which habitually we knock on the doors of the senses; they lack different parts and disposition, and without these preliminaries, it is impossible to proceed to the act of making effigies. Some things are of a kind that in one part occupies a middle ground; these are things that in a certain sense refer, and are referred; they are called indices. We therefore indicate not only those things that can be effected, imagined, and exemplified, such as examples, images, and effigies; but also those that express and are expressed, such as sigils, notes, and characters. Thus it is not rash to say that in this enumeration, indices fall into a middle place.

XIV

The species, form, simulacrum, example, and apparition of Hermes, therefore, show us Hermes himself. Notes, characters, and sigils show us the substance, essence, goodness, justice, and wisdom of Hermes. That which recalls Hermes to our minds in both ways, and those things which are said to belong to Hermes,

---

76. A common Renaissance trope portrays Nature as the mother of the arts.

are properly called indices. These combine images and notes in one, and by them we show and indicate at the same time. This can be seen manifested in the demonstrative pronouns: of Mercury and virtue alike we say "this simulacrum," "this sign," "that note," and "that similitude."

XV

Considering this, remember that this art is unable to achieve its ends except by means of things that are sensed, formed, figured, and contracted in time and place. Why this happens in all other mental techniques is expressed in the first volume of *The Great Key*. It is not possible, however, to communicate all things by images; since many of the things that are to be memorized can neither be imagined nor made into effigies, nor are they similar to anything that can be linked indirectly to an image or effigy; examples are terms, uses, hypostases, mind, and other things of this genus; but instead, things that signify can be expressed by signs, and things that can be imagined by images. It is so that they are not passed over by the mind that images are no less to be joined to signs, as signs to images.

XVI

Out of a defect of connection comes a certain infirmity in using this art, which is that in many cases, ordered species do not occur, and this does not only happen from the source that our predecessors have considered. This is because the sense of sight sometimes fails because of the excellence of the light, the obscurity of the darkness, the greatness of the multitude, the dispersal by distance, and other things of the same kind, in the places in which things are accustomed to be. For this reason, just as a biting dog may be hit with a stone as well as a stick, those who do not understand the true source of this distinction find fault with another.

We, however, to whom it has been given to find and perfect this art, have no need for material places (verified by the external senses), nor do we draw up in order a list of ordered places to be memorized, constructed purely of imagination.[77] We presume to have succeeded in this so far, that whatever the ancients considered, taught, and ordained in this art (insofar as these are explained in

---

77. Two of the most common ways of organizing memory images in Bruno's time.

those of their writings that have come into our hands) is not necessary to our invention, which is an invention in the pregnant mode to which *The Great Key* is appropriate. Meanwhile, however, we return to the dignity of this consideration.

XVII

Fame is the consideration of the natural by a proportional consideration of the same, which respects not form alone, nor material alone, which by nature is marked with a name; but formed matter, and material form joined to matter, by which that work is accomplished that is properly called nature. This is that bond which, when it is lacking, no work that nature is capable of performing can possibly be done; much the less can it be done by art, which follows in nature's footsteps; if it is permitted to dream that something may be less than what is less than nothing, this may be true of art, which not only treats nature as its prime subject, but the natural as its proximate subject.

Since all art therefore requires, for its consideration of elements, material reasons suitable for its work, and harmonious forms (of which the general goal of all is to make some new form in some subject), thus in this art, which shares its reasons with the reasons of writing in general, and with an excellent mode of proportion, proportioned by two species of manifestation of the same. There is intrinsic painting, which produces images of things and deeds to be remembered. There is also intrinsic writing, which is ordered by reason and words, and allots signs, notes and characters; even in subjective images. I am not influenced by what is commonly said, either of memory of things, or of the retention of them by ordered forms they call images.

XVIII

Pictures (the term that is properly used in this art) have as their prime subject that on which they are painted, such as walls, stones, and the like. They have as their proximate subject that by which these things are colored, and they have for forms the things drawn in the same colors. Writing has for its prime subject paper, used as a place on which to write. It has for its proximate subject minium, and has for forms those drawn from among written characters. In the same way this art admits as its object a twofold subject: the prime, which is the place, and the proximate, which is appropriate to it, without adjects. Potentially it also admits a duplex subject, that is memory, and imagination in general, in one place, and the species of imaginable or thinkable things in general, in the other place; and it admits as form the intention and collation of the species that exist in one subject, to the species that exist in the other subject. As with painting and writing, which form their material, adapting them to organons; in the same way, in this art, instruments of figuration are not lacking.

The Art of Memory
Part Two

 THREEFOLD CONSIDERATION of this art is therefore necessary at the beginning. The first part is to consider what, and of what quality, its subjects ought to be. The second part is to teach how and in what way its forms ought to appear. The third is to teach the adaptation of the organon, and its medium, in order to develop skill in the practitioner's soul: all of which is set forth perfectly in the beginning of *The Great Key*. Still, so that this book not be truncated and left imperfect in itself (for it is indeed convenient, in transmitting such subordinate disciplines as these, to inquire into the first principles of the art; insofar as the principles that differentiate them are connected to other species, they naturally migrate to the beginning of subordinate sciences), in the third of the three parts of this handbook we will explain the ordering thereof.

The first part concerns the material or the subject. The second concerns the form or the adject. The third concerns the instrument by virtue of which they are made effective, and whence the causes, effective genus, and instrument become the same.

On Subjects

I

First of all, then, the subject is an extension of the technique, or an opening ordained to the imaginative faculty. It belongs to the kind of receptacle that is filled from the windows of the soul. It is divided into distinct parts, so that it can receive all things seen and heard in their proper order, and retain them at will in the soul. This definition relates to the common subject, of common forms, out of the common art that has been handed down to our time from antiquity.

The prime subject, however, is one of the principles of *The Great Key*.[78] By it the chaos of the imagination is made tractable, the power of thinking is brought back into balance, and be heard in such a way as to produce order and image. Thus all the members, from the first to the last, are happily able to present those things that are continually perceived by the eyes and ears, such as an unfamiliar tree or animal, or some newly encountered view of the world.

This is not at all different from the chaos that can be seen when clouds are blown by a wind outdoors; by the different impulses and proportions of the wind, the clouds can take on infinite and varied figures and forms. This prime subject therefore stands forth as happy and noble, and to experience it is better than any power can judge. It is true enough that from *The Great Key* one may call forth anything that can be called forth; still, it is not given to everyone to reach Corinth.[79] We therefore return now to the subject, as defined in the first way.

II

Any given subject consists of material parts, and is therefore material. Thus it does not deceive the faculty of sight, insofar as the subject may be contemplated by the imaginative faculty as being of the visual order, or using the same parts and principles, as in monsters, and numberless new metamorphoses which may be taken apart, and the parts regarded as though with a fixed gaze. These parts in their combinations are not allowed in the more material subjects, the art of which is true art, and the faculty a true faculty.

---

78. That is, the system of *The Great Key* rests on a specially designed general memory image that provides a framework into which all other memory images are fitted.

79. A proverb derived from Christian scripture (*II Corinthians* 10:14) meaning that not everyone can expect to achieve some very good thing—in this case, of course, access to Bruno's secret book. The rest of this section of the book explains how to practice the art of memory without access to the "prime image."

III

In constituting subjects, it is necessary to preserve the ratio between greatness and smallness, relative to human size and perceptive capacity. Between intensity and remission, relative to the limits of the senses. Between past and future, relative to the present moment. Between excessive and deficient parts, relative to the integrity of the whole thing that is present. Between distance and closeness, relative to the capacity for motion. Between the beginning and the end, relative to whatever is moved by natural motion.

IV

Of these the first is very common to subjects, because however much they may be extended, the imagination is able to comprehend this in its folds, and to add any quantity you like to what is placed before the eyes, but it is not permitted to subtract anything. The second is common, and consists of adding all the parts of the known universe. The third is less common, and may be called political. The fourth is specific to individual subjects, and may be considered economic. The fifth more specific, and is the division into four or the division into five. The last is most specific, and is the atom, and the atom not in a simple sense, but in its genus. Of these modes, the first excludes itself from being used in the present art. We know, however, of a way in which the infinite may be reduced into a single place, and multiplied in the same.

V

This also involves a twofold way of working, animate and inanimate. The animate, when substantive subjects appear illustrated and with their insignia, with adjects, and move about according to some adventitious form. Inanimate things are brought forth in voids and empty spaces. Be careful, therefore, that you do not attempt this with vulgar things. Leave the void to the void, or you will hope in vain to practice this art as I have; as is said, the walls shout, and stones will give their voices.[80]

---

80. A reference to *Luke* 19:40.

VI

Commit general things to general things; the less general to the less general; the specific to the specific; the more and most specific to the more and most specific. Here you have a theme for consideration that will not only make you free of all fear of forgetting, but indeed will give you a more perfect way of imaging and writing, as well as a method of methods for invention and disposition,[81] and doing so more quickly and securely. Here you have, in this mode, the first of the foundations of *The Great Key*.[82]

VII

All things natural, physical, and technical, admit of form. Forms that produce images are proportionate to their images in quantity, and for this reason you will remember that nature herself cries out, prescribing that species have their greater and lesser limits, and insofar as they undertake to obey the law, it is not permitted that any amount of matter should take any form.

What is considered the upper limit of measure is referred to the ancients, who reflected a great deal on forms or their adjects, and were accustomed most often to assign them to subjects. There is no crystalline limit visible on high[83] against which your intention can strike, nor draw back beneath those limits, insofar as they move less swiftly to the inner eye, or at least are rendered more convenient.

You should be careful in making images not to do any of the things that should be avoided in external writing; thus I do not suggest that one subject should be put right up against other subjects, nor that you should neglect to distinguish proper limits and intervals; nor that you should mix proper figurations with alien ones; for then they will block your conjectures, and prevent you from attaining any other. As letters that are written over letters and seals that are made over seals, these either destroy each other or at least confound each other, no less with subjects than with the things annexed and connected

---

81. Invention and disposition are the first two of the five classical parts of rhetoric; Bruno is pointing out here that his method is not simply about memory, the fourth part of rhetoric.

82. This suggests that the memory image central to the *Great Key* is an image of the universe.

83. A poetic simile; Bruno used the image of the supposed crystalline spheres of heaven, which were rejected by Copernicus, to equate the unlimited space of the Copernican universe with the unlimited potential he saw in his art of memory.

to them; but if your images are continuous, or contiguous, and not set apart by an interval of appropriate breadth, I implore you to recognize that you will run into confusion.

VIII

In the same way, subjects should be chosen so that they have definite means, lengths, heights, breadths, and differences of their outward limits, and other habitudes differentiating themselves from one another. For all virtues are presented by nature, and affect the eye either externally or internally, by their colors as well as the location of their light sources and the differences of their outward limits, proceeding from the principles of perspective, both optical and catoptical, to achieve the most wonderful appearances. If the reasoning mind creates subjects that do not possess these properties by themselves, the thinking process (as I have indicated) attempts to put them in, either by adding something external to the subjects, or adding something appropriate to them, so that by congruent formations, one or the other is able to provide the materials. By subtraction, a statue of Mercury is made out of a rock. By addition, a ship is built from wood. By compression and division, an effigy is made of wax. By drawing things out, a figure is made from lines. By alteration, wine becomes vinegar. Similar changes are wrought in other things by commingling, separation, solution, consequence, and continuation for the changing of forms, and so universally among all the mutable things of nature.

IX

It also must not be forgotten that subjects ought to be considered, when they are viewed in internal cogitation, in a way that is proportioned to the gaze of the eyes. In the outer world, sensible[84] things are not sensed when they are inherent in the organs of sense, and sensible things that are extremely far from the organs of sense lack the power to be sensed. A book may not be read if it is either too close to the eyes, or too far from them, and in the same way, in placing the internal gaze, you should so regulate matters that as its faculties are placed at a middle distance relative to its power of extension, that it may form and shape the object itself.

---

84. Sensible things: that is, things that are of a nature to be perceived by the senses.

It is as important to remember that subjects that are believed and memorized are naturally easier to remember, when they are brought to mind by considering them. From this consideration proceeds an impoverishment of memory, as some believe they have formed a subject, or that they gaze attentively at what is figured, when actually they do not.[85] For one thing is placed under another thing, as though they wrote in shadow, or under a veil.

X

The spacing of subjects determines their continuity and their distribution. In order to distinguish them, it should be considered that the space between one subject and another should be just so much as will seem to be abolished and deleted. On the contrary, where there is a continuum and so much uniform space that it goes beyond what is enough, its natural effect is to join the subjects together. You ought to order your positions one after another, and conceive the subjects as marked with adjects. What, then, prevents the ancient imagination from returning here, so that it may happen that I touch it anew? Indeed, this imagination, which could be put in place of truth, cannot be lightly had or lightly formed, for cogitation is inherent in it, insofar as they are customary to you, they are in no wise seen to be different from truer things. In this, however, you may excel to some degree by practice.

XI

Reviewing the subjects is to be done repeatedly, insofar as it brings advantage, which the present method is able to do. Surely you are not ignorant of the way that those who are accustomed to read much do so more swiftly than can be readily believed by those who must pick through words a letter at a time, seeing that writing is composed of letters? In the same way, practice leads to a more perfect way of doing which is without thought; which is achieved by practicing solely, and very intently, upon single parts and elements, which are repeated and guided by thought. The most perfectly practiced guitarists[86] act solely by habit, not by thinking about their guitar-playing; others, by means of touch alone, can

---

85. That is, it is easy in practicing the art of memory to think that you have a clear image of something familiar, when no such image has been formed.

86. The guitar was already a popular instrument in Bruno's time, especially in Spain and in Spanish possessions such as the part of Italy where Bruno grew up.

achieve the same thing; those who have not practiced, to that measure they are considered beginners, and as much more so, as they have to think about their playing. This shows the power of practice even to the vulgar. The way that mere water is able to wear a hole in hard marble or iron shows this to the perceptive. Still, is anything concerning this matter more abundantly manifest? We do not neglect to discuss it, not at all indeed because it is not manifest enough, but because the subject of this proposition is worth any amount of trouble. They know that one of the working rules of the ancients is to set subjects far apart from one another, and to do the same with very many of them; in this way, they can bring them forth to expression by one act of cogitation, no less swiftly and exactly as if they read them on paper. To those who are unskilled, and those who first gird themselves for the work, this commonly appears incredible; indeed, it brings the opposite conviction. Still, what if this is done by the ancient arts, and we see it to be done every day: which, I say, can be brought about with the very briefest delay by practice? These arts will appear to you greater, better, and more accurate, in three or four revolutions of the Moon; which six revolutions of the Sun would otherwise be needed to accomplish. Thus we find the way to commit to memory any subjects whatsoever one at a time, and to retain each one of them in its proper place, and in greater scale and number, which is demonstrable by the arcana of *The Great Key*. What, how many, and in what way it will touch upon these things, others will see for themselves, so that they are able to judge rightly of both.

XII

You may therefore behold the variety that is so eminently brought forth by Nature. The members of the world are diverse; diverse are the forms in the members of the world; diverse are the figures in individual forms; no one olive is exactly the same shape as any other; no one man is exactly like any other. Thus all things differing are of distinct capacity, and one by one, and all by all, are properly set apart by their own differing limits. Thus you should try whatever will conform to Nature in all her diversity, in mode of subsistence, magnitude, form, figure, habit, condition, limit, and place, and as frequently as you can, put in differences in acting, being acted upon, growing, seizing, subtracting, adding, and changing in other modes, as we have said. The terms being and one are said interchangeably; whatever is not one, is not a being, and every single thing we must therefore perceive as a unity, because what is proper to it is bounded by what is different from it. Uniformity nauseates all the senses, both when one particular quality is repeated until it no longer delights, and when one and the same thing lasts unchanged for an immoderate time; for the senses suffer when they are affected by one and the same mode exactly. This has not escaped those who consider the very swift flowing of all natural things; as it is impossible to step in the same river twice or, indeed, even once.

XIII

From this depends the affectivity of subjects. By "affectivity" I mean that which acts on the faculty of the emotions, which among other things is produced by the allurement or stimulus of variety, by the intrinsic nature of the subjects, and is indicated by their position. For this reason it is thought appropriate by some to add a certain subject to the principal subjects, so that even if these do not have affectivity of themselves, they would receive it from these others, as though by the addition of a graft. But why? The more affectivity that subjects themselves give out and are given, the more powerful and subtle the effects with which they move the imagination, and enter and reenter the palace of memory. Thus the spurs, the cleverness, and the goads;[87] thus the seasonings, thus the forgetting while they try to remember, repeat, recapitulate, and resume, as though by diversity or alternation, or by the better means which I propound; or by all these things in diverse manners, they hope to summon the spirit of memory. This latter comes very easily to those who practice with a mind as little disturbed as possible; otherwise, the more the disturbance becomes and the more heated it is, the more they tend to confusion. How many are the kinds of virtue in affectivity, and in what way they can be called forth, preserved, and varied, will be presented in no little detail in the book *The Great Key*.

On Adjects

I

Adjects, or general forms, are therefore defined by subjects, whether these are physical, technical, or imaginative subjects, so that by the skillful application of thought, something that is to be expressed and signified may be presented,

---

87. That is, in Bruno's view, it is because of the inadequate affectivity of the subjects they use that other systems of memory are forced to rely on tricks of various kinds.

portrayed, noted, or indicated in the similitude of writing and painting. In this, reason respects the common forms that have come down to our times from antiquity. Its form is that which is derived from fundamentals in *The Great Key*; it is produced and explained according to the order of the forms of thought, in statues, or the microcosm; or generally disposed in the other forms of architec-

Figure 5. *Primary Figure*[88]

ture; so that whatever can be spoken may be written internally, or portrayed by drawing upon the chaos of the imagination, which admits of all metamorphoses. The type thereof is not only described here, but we have presented it for your consideration as well.

II

There is chaos in your nature primordially, which does not exclude the order and series of elements and numbers; this must be understood not only in the sense that what is unformed may be formed, but also that it is necessary to conceive what is formable in due order. As you can see, it is distinguished by diverse intervals in it and in its parts which form the whole figure; which are designated by its creator as elements. The letter A, by means of the unformed numbers and elements, runs through the circuit and the radius. It impresses another figure by Aries, another by Taurus, others in their turn by the remaining signs; another by Aries when Saturn returns to it, another when Mars revisits it, and so with the others; and still another without any of the planets. In this way the subject may

---

88. No figure is presented in the Latin text at this point. The primary figure intended is very likely the image of the universe on which the *Great Key* is based.

be formed and reformed to an infinite degree, either by its numbers or its elements, or drawn in diverse ways by those things that move and affect it. This is what it is to bring form to formless chaos, or to form the same with forms; you may refer either to things that give form or to things that receive it, it makes no difference to the proposition.

Nonetheless there is that which remains unchanged, and submits; to the extent that it submits, and is formed, it is considered to be as feminine as water[89] and wholly formless, so that it may be formed by influences from any source. It is according to the common judgment the most perfect chaos if it is composed of unordered things conjured from thin air, but this cannot be used at all. That which is useful must be obedient to the numbers and elements of memory, which are disposed according to a certain order, from which come moving and shaping principles; while other things that are to be remembered are able to accept forms. These, however, are (as you will see) so disposed by order, that they are never able at any time to occupy the same circuit or radius, whether according to element or number. Many other most excellent things can be drawn forth from this figure, but this is not the place for that to be done. Whether it is appropriate to consider doing this I have not yet decided, but this much I affirm. The one thing I would wish to say is that if you were to contemplate that figure according to the reasons explained here, you would be able to acquire the art of figuration to such a degree that it would confer upon you that which would wondrously help not memory alone, but that as well as every other power of the soul.

III

It must therefore be noted first, concerning adjects, that their proper proportions are between excess and diminution, intensification and remission, past and future, distance and propinquity, appropriate to man's size, or the half thereof, and to his gaze, and in the present time, in which memory ought to be.

---

89. The elements were gendered in Renaissance thought: fire and air were masculine, water and earth feminine.

IV

Of adjects, some are animate, and they are able to act simultaneously as efficient, adjacent, and operative organons. Others are inanimate, and those belonging to this category act as adjacent and operative organons only. Of animate adjects, in turn, some participate in reason, and so are apt to every kind of action and passion, and also have a neutral mode. Others are without reason, and concerning them (as is well manifest) there is not enough agreement in the world.

V

Furthermore, some adjects are natural and others are artificial, some pass from the external senses to the internal senses, while others are formed in the internal senses themselves, of which the species are Form, Similitude, Image, Figure, Example, Character, and Sign, distinguished according to the formal significations that are revealed in the considerations of *The Great Key*.

VI

Concerning magnitude,[90] adjects are customarily made commensurate with their subjects, just as occurs in natural things, for otherwise they would easily be lost, and the visual imagination either blunted or scattered. It takes a long time indeed to write in very small letters on an ample page, and it is more difficult to do. Because if its mass, in turn, a tree that fills or exceeds the space around it does not present a clear figure to the observer. For these reasons, we have tested a method, by means of a certain industriousness, whereby a certain moderate and secret subject of the visual imagination is offered in addition; this is combined with the form of another adject by which it is customarily held and accompanied, as the archer carries an arrow, the scribe a pen, and the shoemaker an awl. These have so much virtue in connecting, linking, preceding, accompanying and following, that they make invisible things visible, intelligible things apparent through the sensible universe, and things difficult to grasp easily comprehended.

---

90. Magnitude (or quantity), quality, and relation, the subject of this and the following two sections, are three of the ten basic categories from Aristotle's *Categories*, a textbook studied throughout the western world in Bruno's time.

VII

Concerning quality, whether they be visible or imaginary things, adjects must be able to set thought into motion, whether by being something admirable, frightening, funny, sad, pleasant, hateful, abominable, probable, wonderful, prodigious, hoped for, suspected, or anything else that bursts in upon our most powerful feelings, and bring themselves along with the feelings. Thus you should be careful not to stray from a sober understanding of the mode of our precepts, in which we enumerate the species of adjects, that is, signs, insignia, characters, and sigils.[91] You should modify all of these by all that has been discussed under the things pertaining to quantity, that your eye may be fixed in contemplation on that which is presented for consideration in *The Great Key*: inasmuch as nothing is to be admitted to memory from the senses and the imagination except by way of the cognitive faculty.

VIII

Concerning relation, adjects must not be applied to subjects as though by accident, as though they happened to be thrown together; rather, what is referred to should be comprehended so as to be comprehensible; garments should be things that are proper to be worn, and protections to protect; each is connected to the other in such a way that nothing can slip in between them. Every part of one should be related to every part of another, as pertinent, or as belonging to what is pertinent; ordered or disordered, resistant or compliant, and so on universally, so that each concept is connected to the other concept. What adject could conceive so royal a dignity when separated from any subject? Thus adjects are understood together with their subjects, like letters carved into stone, rather than fluttering about in the wind, or being confused, as happens to figures written in the sand.

IX

Adjects are also understood as acting in a subject, and in individual subjects, or to be acted on by subjects, or in subjects. I say that every action or passion is to be considered vivifying, since by any motion the inner vision, which is as asleep, is roused as though by being shaken—wandering, going over, going under,

---

91. In Renaissance writings the latter two terms were typically used for magical symbols.

going to, going from, going with, ascending, descending, meeting, departing, avoiding, or fleeing; or with some subject, adjects bring, strike, push, exclude, deprive, lead, overturn, bend, vex, throw, twist, drop, demolish, break, erect, raise, uproot, stretch, scratch, clean, remove, empty, or drain. None of this may be done unless adjects are annexed and fixed to subjects, but the more fixed they are, the better; for the ability to make all these changes is founded on fixity and perseverance. You should not, however, give up hope of achieving this stability, for continuous motion does not lack its own stability, insofar as it is continuous; it is for this reason that the poet calls Fortune constant in her inconstancy.[92] This will serve equally well with variety, multitude, speed and slowness; nor are these lacking conditions pertaining to the quality of adjects.

X

As in subjects, so in adjects, uniformity is to be avoided. This should be done as much as possible, for having a variety of things to choose from, as explained above, is consonant with nature. Thus:

> *Per tanto variar natura è bella.* ("Through all her changes, Nature is lovely.")

It is permissible to apply the same adject to different subjects, so long as the adject alone, and over the range of its applications, implies differing actions, and has different species according to the habitudes of the subjects.

XI

Adjects may thus be held by several subjects in common, when this is convenient, but it is necessary to follow the divisions among subjects, so that each of them pertained to one subject, and not be included among those that pertain to another; they should avoid all continuity, connection, crowding, and admixture. When the adjects of diverse subjects are permitted actions and changes here and there, it is as though they were in someone else's hands, and busy with other business, so that you call them to your assistance in vain.

---

92. This image is from *The Consolation of Philosophy* by Boethius.

On the Organon

I

There remains to be discussed the organon, which according to our proposition is something that the soul can use. Without taking action, it is sufficient for the organon to have a complete understanding of the forms that are to be induced, and to grasp the reasons according to which the subjects are formed; for it is indeed true in this work that where opportunity permits, that which is produced by acting on the forms of the subjects, which is the basis for the value of the work, is not to be omitted, insofar as it is essential; again, we must consider of what kind the organon ought to be, and in what way it ought to be put to use.

II

Nine things unite to further memorization and recollection: *intention*,[93] which is from some sense perception, which may be extrinsic or intrinsic, among those that are moved by the object; *provocation of the imagination*, where a movement of the senses either directly or indirectly awakens the imagination; *passive movement of the imagination*, by which it is driven to investigate; *active movement of the imagination*, by which it then investigates; *scrutiny*, by which the imagination investigates according to the intention; *image*, inasmuch as this produces a memorable species; *intention of the image*, which is the reason by which the thing to be remembered is made present, while other things are excluded; *presentation of the intention*, by which the intention is made present; and *judgment*, by which the intention of the image is apprehended.

III

Among all these, that which we call scrutiny or discernment (inasmuch as by it thought inquires and discerns) may easily be determined to be assigned as an instrument to reason, because we call it by this latter name commonly; right up to our own time, however, it has not received proper consideration, and it lacks a proper and popular name. This lack of a rational name and consideration is a barrier in the way of invention, because the foundation upon which reminscence and memory are formed is hidden away in the profound blindness

---

93. The italics are not in the original; I have added them to help bring clarity to Bruno's prose.

of dense darkness. It is therefore this instrument in the faculty of cognition, similar to a stick in our hand (which you are able to grasp by giving it a name or, better still, a reason by which the name should be given) by which what is thrown together in a heap may by us be divided, broken up, and dispersed, just as a selected chestnut may be taken from the midst of acorns, or from among its fellow chestnuts.

IV

This instrument may be known through its action. It has a double virtue, that is, of conservation and remembrance: which (as they say) are one thing, distinguished according to reason; and both of these from imagination, as I see it. The virtue of conservation is found at the limits of the memorative and imaginative virtues, as though it were their neighbor. Remembrance may be distinguished from imagination, since by it the intention of an imaginable form may be comprehended even when the imaginable form is not present, and thereby the form is not deprived of its intention. It happens thus that we may retain many things at once, even if we cannot imagine them all. Herein it acts as an instrument to discern, separate, and order, or (if it is permissible to speak more exactly) it is that by which discretion, separation, and ordering are done.

In this way it is set apart from cogitation, in that it provides a consideration of many things as one, that is, one imagined thing or an image of one retained out of many, drawn out into a proposition. And as it is said to comprehend the imaginative, as though it were a picture painted on a wall, and remembrance of that picture retains the intention; so that this organon by turns departs and approaches, or more properly makes a report, and applies the one to the other; and if these are linked to one another, they enter into an embrace like the links of a chain or the equivalent. Therefore, as Nature herself brought this connection down to our own times, Art emulated her by the order of places; where it was not possible to connect one thing to another, they were ordered one after another, but not properly, I say, nor according to reason; but appropriated simply on account of their present position, and by this connection, as though by the application of extraneous images, was to be brought to remembrance.

Thus the office of scrutiny is that unities (by which I mean many individual things; I concede this much to the correctors of words) are taken according to some symbolism and by these disposed in order. While a hundred eggs taken one at a time, and assigned diverse numbers, as 1, 2, 3, 4, 5, 6, 7, 8, 9, and so on successively would be completely useless, and would soon form groups, and occurring in a confused manner, would reach the point that they would interfere with one another; someone could move eggs out of one heap and into another with a stick, taking some and leaving others, so that one by one he brings them into order; thus cogitation, quickly distinguishing itself from the other powers of the mind, determinately chooses one after another by this virtue of scrutiny.

Here is a locus[94] for consideration by similitude, how in the same way as in a crowd, the eggs receive, from the memory of numerical order, an order that they would not otherwise have. Thus we may easily find the genus of arts by which things we have heard or seen, forming numbers congruent to the same genus, being themselves ordered by number, we conceive the order of things perceived by the senses accordingly since, knowing how to number things, we learn to remember very easily. This method of forming numbers for all things is one of the ways our method stands out among all others. The theory thereof is in the book *The Great Key*, where semimathematical numbers are discussed. I believe I have displayed enough of this to inventive minds in this place, where, if we have not hinted enough, we have at least said enough to provide a clear congruence of places. This has been considered by us in respect of the few, that they may have an advantage, but not for all.

V

There are thus a certain number of scrutinies, by which cogitation comes into contact in its own way with the species it conserves, having in itself the ability of dividing, separating, collecting, applying, preserving, forming, ordering, and bringing together into a chosen unity. Scrutinies are said to be numerous, because there is no convenient genus into which they can all be gathered together. Further, the number is such that there is none other by which the same memorability can be implanted, or obtained; notwithstanding that we would not perceive it by means of any other figure, nor by the same, defined according to any agreement, of the sort that in memorizing is necessarily concurrent with the principle (such places having power not in that they are places, nor because they are imagined, but because they contain latent number in them on account

---

94. A *locus*, place, or topic, in the jargon of Renaissance rhetoric, was a theme for reflection that was used for the purpose of rhetorical invention. Bruno is offering his metaphor of eggs for this purpose.

of their order) concerning which we explain two different reasons (of which each draws to itself the next closest genus, and the other draws another so that we may by this agreement have the best results).

Numbers are most clearly denominated according to their ordinal position, and thus differ from numbers denominated by their cardinal value.[95] It is to the latter that we refer when we ask, "How many eggs are there?" To those denominated by their ordinal position, we refer when we ask, "In what order did the eggs arrive?" With them, we could do as well by asking, "Which number is this egg? Which number is that one?" and it would be said to be different according to ordinal number. A question about number can be taken in either way, for if someone responds by saying "first," "second," or "third," then the first, second, or third occurs, or can be made to occur, in order. By the second in order, the smallest difference is specified, rather than by the first.[96] This belongs to the practice rather than the theory of ordinal numbers, which consists not in logic but in use. For indeed use appears twice: that is, first, with respect to a particular person and a particular determinate habit, as things happen to be recorded by ingenuity, reason, and intelligence; whence the person knows that this is to be said, this is to be brought forth, this to follow thereafter, and after it something else in rational order. In this, properly speaking, reminiscence is said to take place, and differs thus from memory according to a famous distinction. Second, without respect to persons, but rather with something that may be said to be a more absolute reason (though, granted, it is not truly absolute), which happens to us when we are able to remember something that is not at all intellectual, such as this passage concerning Charon according to Merlin—[97]

"Parts of the land are shaken wholly into ruin."

—or others of the same kind, in which there cannot be a cogitative act, nor any act of distinct virtue, by which the memory is able to exist; still, it is manifestly

---

95. I have had to paraphrase here, for Bruno uses two Latin terms—*quotuitas* and *quotitas*—that have no exact English translation. The point at issue, however, is the difference between ordinal numbers ("first, second, third") and cardinal numbers ("one, two, three"); the former, Bruno suggests, are easier to remember.

96. That is, in a series of numbered things, such as points on a line, the smallest interval between them is between the first and second; the individual point takes up no interval by itself.

97. A passage from one of the many prophecies attributed to Merlin in circulation in Bruno's time. Merlin's prophecies were as popular then as those of Nostradamus are today.

true of reminiscence, however, that there is some manifest difference between one and another.

When this application is not referred to the memory of that which it is to receive and retain (as we have said, and will prove by demonstration in the doctrine of *The Great Key*), nor to what is generally called fantasy (inasmuch as it includes in its connotation what is commonly described as common sense), which is none other than that which stands before the particular and external senses in the mode appropriate to them, either in whole or in part. Nor, certainly, is it of the cogitative virtue, which is of the apprehending cognitive faculties, among those which belong alongside examples of perceivable and knowable things. What, then, is that inner power by which those sounds that are perceived by the ear and reported to the common sense,[98] as sounds wholly naked, are able to enter into memory? If it is cogitative, certainly (though it is hardly permissible to define another internal power, equal with the cogitative power of memory, and inserting itself next thereto) it is by no means only cogitative, but equipped with scrutiny, by which not only those things that can be touched by the hands, but also those to which the hand is, as it were, unable to extend, are admitted among those things that prompt the memory. Among these, certainly, this instrument must necessarily belong, and the aspects of it that are not obvious stand in the way of many discoveries.

VI

The genus of acts that follow on scrutiny comprises five species: Applying, Forming, Altering, Unifying, and Ordering, which have been noted by very few people; as not all know well what they see and hear, and in what way they see and hear, and what it is by which they see and hear; and in the same way, not all of those who apply, form, alter, unify, and order, know in what way these proceed, and what it is by which they proceed. To notice this it is enough for the soul to reason in a certain state of universality and confusion, but this will not be enough to reveal the powers, faculties, and organs thereof; nor would we desire to appear before us something that would be more deeply flawed than

---

98. In Renaissance psychology, the common sense was that aspect of consciousness in which the reports of the individual senses were combined to produce mental perceptions of things.

a certain thing of the Arabs who are learned in the Peripatetic school, and by which some are influenced.[99]

But if we wish to set all of this in order, we would begin with the greatest matter, and the most difficult to communicate; especially since I see very few philosophers in our time that hold opinions corresponding to what has just been said; I pass by those other names, brought forth by new inventions and considerations, that have done so much damage; for this reason, that "finished goods become raw materials,"[100] and also because this matter is directed mostly by practice rather than the appearance of necessity. Those things that most particularly are to be noted concerning scrutiny, therefore, we now introduce according to their proper order.

VII

It should be noted, for practical application, that the faculties just noted retain analogy and order among themselves, so that the outer senses may direct themselves toward bodies; fantasy toward simulacra of bodies; imagination toward the single intentions of simulacra; and intellect, in turn, toward the common natures of single intentions and inward incorporeal relationships. From this it follows by analogy (as I have shown elsewhere) that just as art stands forth as that which attracts, draws, and binds the external senses, so it is that which entices and most tenaciously conquers them.

Why did birds gather around the grapes that Zeuxis painted?[101] Why was the Venus sculpted by Praxiteles so hard to keep from the hands of the lustful?[102] Because a certain artificial form applies to its subject in such a way that it expresses them more intensely and exquisitely than the thing itself; some of them serve as a basis by which species creep into the mind principally, and (so to speak) capitally, when they enter by the senses. It is possible, as I have already said, that this principle is common to all things; still, it is clear that it does not

---

99. Muslim scholars in the Middle Ages studied and greatly expanded on the works of Aristotle; I have not, however, been able to determine which part of their teaching Bruno references here.

100. That is, the finished work of one scholar or generation becomes the raw material for the next.

101. Zeuxis was a famous Greek painter, who was said to have painted a bunch of grapes so realistic that birds gathered around them, trying to eat them.

102. Another famous Greek artist, Praxiteles was said to have carved a nude marble statue of Aphrodite (Venus) so lifelike and alluring that it had to be guarded to keep men from fondling it.

affect all things to the same degree; thus the more apt and timely is the instrument (for example, the body), the clearer the souls will be.

VIII

Clearer souls that are more exposed to divine Ideas receive the forms of objects more intensely, just as one who sees more acutely, more easily and aptly discerns them. Forms in material bodies are held to be no different in this from the images of the divine ideas. When these latter are received by the inward senses of humanity, what better name could they be entitled to have than the shadows of the divine ideas, as they are apart from the reality of natural things, just as natural things are apart from the truths of metaphysics? Indeed, of these species in the recesses of the intellect, we would more readily believe that they are made immediately by conversion to that light which acts in our intelligence, and which is brought in from that which is outward by the inward sense through the mediation of the forms of physical things.

Still, we will try one set of things in one way, and another in another. It is best to proceed in both ways at the same time, and avoid becoming entangled in contradictions; and how this is done, we have demonstrated elsewhere; and you, if you are versed in the most common philosophy, will be able to determine it for yourself. But if you will not increase the light that shines from this eye by applying yourself, how can you hope to draw in through it the other powers of the soul that you are capable of knowing? Is this called anything else but having closed eyes? What else is having your eyes closed than to be turned, as they say, toward the shadow of death? Is it not the truth of things, handed down to the mouths of the vulgar, that so many equate "to close one's eyes" with "to be dead"?

IX

With regard to formation, which follows application, it should first be noted that its whole power is placed in the mode and species of its application. The power of apprehending in general has this in common with matter: that in itself, and by itself, it is nothing but a hollow container; none of the elements has in itself any odor, or flavor, or color; but it is well known that in their coming together, in diverse orders and grades, they produce all color, flavor, and odor. Fire sheds light only when it is applied to other bodies, and when placed on and near various bodies in diverse ways, it shines more or less brightly.[103] The resulting radiance is not possessed by fire in itself, nor by the other body in itself, but it is in both by virtue of application. By this you have in similitude the formation both of intellect and of memory which is improved by application; in this way, better than in the preceding, application stands out, and the greatest efficacy thereof consists in large part in the proper guidance of scrutiny.

X

There are those who claim that forms that may be easily reduced are those that belong to the imagination and the common sense, being according to them largely corporeal and only a little spiritual. Forms that are difficult to reduce, by contrast, they consider largely spiritual and only a little corporeal. They are persuaded of this because forms that are mostly corporeal remain behind when the common sense distinguishes the spiritual from the corporeal; whence the spiritual contains those forms that are fixed in it, and in particular, it receives with them few outward vestures. From this they infer reciprocally that human beings have souls slow to move, in which the transient perceptions of the senses are fixed, and that these are therefore better for recollection.

All this has a certain easy persuasiveness which borrows its explanatory terms from opinions and writings concerning sleep. They constitute memorative species, some quick, some slow, some tempestuous, some calm; some represented by Martin's horse, some by George's horse, which are not serious enough for discussion and understanding. Let this be grasped by everyone: corporeality never exists simply as corporeality, but more properly you should say that a body exists as a body, and it ought to be understood by anybody that ultimately it may universally be asserted that from corporeality no action proceeds; the lesser derives from the greater, and the least from the greatest, because the body insofar as it is a body does not act.[104] Action is from quality, and that which is more spiritual pertains more to quality, and the incorporeal most of all. As it pleases them thus to understand the words of some very famous men, they are unable to

---

103. This is a commonplace of Renaissance physics: fire sheds no light in its pure form, but only when combined with another element or combination of elements, as when flame is put to wood.

104. Another commonplace of Renaissance philosophy; matter was held to be completely passive, and action in it was caused by the presence of spiritual influences.

keep from running into constant inconveniences, and if you wish to avoid these, know that corporeal things do not act because they are corporeal, but because they endure long and are the vehicles of accidents,[105] which yield information that endures in enduring bodies, and thus is made to endure longer still.

This excuse cannot be taken or retained without being vomited forth in these same words, for it is an opinion suited for a very light stomach. I suggest that the more crude something is, the more obstinate it is, and the more obstinate the more crude. Nor is it a valid objection that when we remain in consideration of a single thing, it is more readily recalled to memory than when it is only lightly considered after it passes; we have experienced no less often that some things heard and seen or considered briefly are recorded forever in memory, while others that are seen and considered for a longer time, and more attentively, are not retained at all. Thus there is no virtue at all in time and corporeality, but rather in their greatest contrary, which is what pertains to bodies. To the contrary, in fact, it is not delay that fixes memories, but the activity of form which delay somehow appears to confer; because some forms are not apt or suited for quick action, or to receive a subject quickly, and thus by delay the action is accomplished.

Where the form is more spiritual, however, it is more active. Thus fire is the most active of the elements, because it is the most spiritual among them, and has the greatest power to turn them into itself, and when provided with matter, all by itself it grows without limit. It is not by being manifold that it acts so much, and it does not do great things on account of being very corporeal, but because of its more intense quality, which is accustomed to maintain its greatness; and its quality (as some of the Platonists noted) if it could be reduced to a part of that magnitude, would become so much more intense that it would act with twice the power; if reduced to the least size, with the greatest power; and if reduced to an atom, with infinite power. From this, it may be considered that the sayings of the philosophers may be called unworthy of consideration.

XI

Thence it appears that it is ignorantly indeed (for it should be noted that this is not without advantage to those who presently see it instituted) that a certain

---

105. Accidents in Renaissance philosophy are factors modifying substances; for example, in "blue water," water is a substance and the color blue is one of its accidents.

horse doctor proposes to the vulgar: not quality, but quantity.[106] This proposition ought to be met with total opposition. Be it noted first of all that such a quality of a virtue be not less than such a quantity, and in much quantity much quality would be conserved; nonetheless action ought never to be referred to matter, and all of it that pertains to the organization of matter; extension is itself set in order (even in its signs) to provide a vehicle for quality and form.

It may nonetheless be accepted as though by the apothecaries, who have this maxim, because they charge according to the quantity which is in weight, number, and measure, whatever the quality of the simples, drugs, and other confections might happen to be; and for that reason, I think, a certain apothecary distinguished among them is well known in our country. "Not quality but quantity" would be consistent with asking about a pig, even though it is not valued for the same things as a horse, whether it has attractive eyes, small ears, a neck drawn back, a broad chest, a projecting face, a mouth lifted up, nimble legs, and so on. Rather, we ask only whether it has long and full sides, and this latter would be just as conveniently referred to a pig as to what is inside an apothecary's shop. "Not quality but quantity," like the loving mother who doted on her daughters and doctored her sons.

XII

Unification and alteration are allowed a twofold action, but they act together; for changing causes unification, and unifying causes change. The reason for this may be made clear in this way. Heraclitus said, "If all beings were to become smoke, the nostrils would distinguish them."[107] We would say, less elegantly, "If everything except foxes were to be turned into chickens, then foxes would never go hungry, since all things would be edible to foxes." Of the powers that convert all things into their own mode, one is the human imagination; of powers that consume and taste in their own mode, one is the human power of cogitation. This kind of conversion is able to attain (though not without the cogitative act) the imagination; as all things committed to memory cannot come back to mind powerfully without the cogitative act of imagination.

---

106. The great slogan of the scientific revolution was already being brandished in Bruno's time.

107. Heraclitus was an early Greek philosopher whose work survives only in fragments.

You may say that it is proper to convert all imagination either into one species, or in several; if they are converted and reformed into one, then there will not be a memory of many things, but of one; if everything were turned into eggs, then not even a wolf[108] would multiply the species of edible things that can be named beyond one, since everything would be edible. If imagination were to be converted and reformed into several species, either finite or infinite: if finite, then either determinate and able to be known or determined, or indeterminate, and then we will be in the same situation we are in already. An infinite number of species would be stupid even to attempt.

It is therefore proper to know that the conversion should not be done in such a way that diversity of substance is eliminated, nor the accidents proper to each thing erased. Rather, each of these should be applied to one convenient form which is affected in the appropriate way, so that one at a time they are put into a memorable order. Just as everything a wolf devours becomes one, so every substance, and everything that applies immediately to substance, goes into one genus of accidents.

Figure 6.

Just as the vowel in the center of the circle, if it be left unnumbered, and the elements are to be imagined as related to it (without forgetting that the vowel

108. The traditional emblem of ravenous hunger.

itself has its own diversity), they all go into a single sound, and depart from it only as, by the application of the vowel, they include its essence with the diversity of the other, that thereby it is more able to enter the same. Thus with one breath, by the appropriate organs in their proper proportions, many diverse sounds are produced. Why, then, should you feel despair and not dispose yourself, and as it were, gird yourself for some of the species to be compared out of the innumerable possibilities, situated in the confines of the imaginative and cogitative faculties, which may be seen in the universe and in books, that they may be put memorably into your soul? This is something we leave to your own efforts, if you are ingenious.

Consider well the remarkable manner of invention practiced by Pan the Arcadian god when he first joined together the reeds of the meadow. Clever folk were accustomed to sound these one at a time with difficulty, but with a single breath, unequal pipes could be played together as one, gathered one at a time and made into a unity, so that they readily stood forth as a single thing.

XIII

As to what pertains to ordering, to the vulgar (to whom minor and modest things are proper) there are propositions depending from it which are considered, by those who are with us, to be more easily explicated than put into practice. Principally, then, reminiscence is said to happen when one motion succeeds another motion by necessity, or one motion is accompanied by another motion, whether it be local, temporal, rational, artificial, or in any other manner of positive relatedness or succession of one thing after another. In this way, indeed, we proceed from the memory of snow to that of winter, and thence to that of cold; thence to shivering, and then to seeking to warm the stomach, and from there to the power of digestion; from that to appetite, and food to digest, strength, and exercise, and so on. In all other things, it works in the same way.

If something has a nature that is without order, however, let it be referred to another order, and rest upon that, which should always be something perceptible to the senses. It was not rashly that a certain thoughtful philosopher said that the order of sensible things is according to its proper nature, and that he did not know what was outside the boundaries of nature. If you ask where order comes from, I will say that it is the progress of things according to the way of nature. What lacks order, I say, has departed from the way of nature. This is what we wish to say about the organon, and pertaining to the organ of scrutiny; if you contemplate these things attentively, nothing will stop you from proceeding straight to the end, and by them you will remove those things that would otherwise close the way leading to the practical applications that follow. We certainly cannot do it for you, nor put under the heading of theory what can only be accomplished by practice itself.

The Art of Memory
Part Three

I

E PROCEED, THEN, to formal operation, that we may go on in order as we have done already, from listing the more elementary and simple things, to considering those that are composed, integral, and perfect.

First, therefore, just as the hand moves pages so that the eyes may look upon the characters inscribed thereon, we propose, before presenting those subjects upon which the memory is to work, to reveal their virtue and efficacy in the following way. A common subject is selected,[109] and first is divided into its major parts, which ought to come after the subject itself in the arrangement of the work; and these major parts may more properly be called subjects themselves.[110] Thence follows subdivision, so that the resulting parts may be limited by one another, and may be ordered by each other, so that they succeed one another according to rules, and in natural or positive contiguity, are divided into still other parts, which are the most specific and individual subjects;[111] and

---

109. This common subject has the same role as the memorized interior of a building in the classical art of memory: it provides the imaginative framework within which all the other mnemonic images find their places.

110. These correspond to the rooms in a building in the classical art of memory.

111. These correspond to the individual places within a memory room. Here as elsewhere, Bruno is taking the specific principles of the classical art and generalizing them so that they may be applied more freely.

these ought to be multiplied between the need for a breadth of more specific subjects, and the convenience of having additional places for memories.

II

Once these are properly disposed and held ready for memory, there should be a catalogue of diverse things that are perceived by the senses, which at first should number twenty-five, then fifty, and finally a hundred, so that gradually, for the benefit of exercise, these may be arranged according to the system you desire; so that it will be seen most clearly what a proper order gives to the natural memory, by means of the subjects which are distributed and applied to it. You should order them for yourself just as though they happened to be written on pages, so that you will be able to proceed from last to first, just as easily as from first to last. In the same way, you may invert the order of reference however you wish, applying to it the places of the things perceived by the senses.

III

In the same way, we proceed from recognizing the efficacy of subjects to the structure of adjects, which are by no means light or fragile foundations supporting the natural memory. There are two kinds of memory, that is, memory of words and memory of things; this is simply an admission of necessity; for there is also a certain other kind, in which the memorative faculty by its own sharpness may be trusted to carry out its own proper function.[112] Because of the more serious difficulties and challenges that have to be faced, we are not accustomed to notice the lesser ones that happen either because the habitual patterns of one of the faculties, when it happens that a proposition and an opinion must be expressed in the first words that come to mind; or because it sometimes happens that we need to call to mind a unique and proper name, and it does not come promptly, as with herbs, trees, minerals, seeds, and other things of that kind, with which it is by no means enough to have the concept alone; or finally because the occasion offers itself of bringing forth words, and we have no idea what to say.

---

112. That is, the natural memory is not divided into memory for things and memory for words; it is only because of the natural memory's weakness that it is necessary to draw this distinction.

IV

The genera by which things rather than words are applied, explained, and woven together, we will declare in another place. Of the genus to which this faculty belongs, however, enough has already been said that it should be easily attained by you; and you also have the best teacher and leader in Nature, who is both within you and around you, and which always illuminates you by means of your own reasoning powers and the objects present to you.[113]

V

Of the modes by which may be applied the many and, indeed, innumerable words that may occur to you while you are busy, which are taught in the *Great Key* (which is indeed the fount of all invention), those which seem more convenient to us in diverse places, we explain in diverse ways. The one way that until our time was used by the ancients we wholly condemn, because it is laborious and requires much practice, nor is it suitable to all purposes.

VI

We must therefore discuss inner reading, compressing its breadth and length, for by dividing and drawing apart words into visual images, more labor would be necessary, and thus, because of the difficulty of the art and the necessity of long exercise, it would repel minds intent on more worthy business. Why should this be necessary? If to the individual subject, by a single adject, may be committed only one letter[114] (out of many), this would require innumerable differences of combination and composition. Concerning this, when this art was first transmitted by the Greeks to the Latins, a certain Greek writer[115] derided the practice of trying to memorize images of individual words, that by these they might be prepared, so that time might not be wasted when there was an

---

113. This section should be taken as a broad hint about the purpose of the thirty intentions and conceptions outlined earlier in the book.

114. Bruno uses the word *elementum* to mean a letter of the alphabet; this was common usage at his time, but may be confusing to modern readers. I have therefore translated it "letter."

115. Bruno's memory has played him false here. The author who decried memory for words is the Latin orator Quintilian, whose treatise on rhetoric is one of the classical sources for the art of memory.

opportunity to study. He saw that there was an infinite multitude of words, and therefore it would be ridiculous to try to find images for them all. To us, however, it is not only possible but easily known, how to be able to have prepared images by which, one by one and in any place whatsoever, I may assign entire words, and do so in many different ways; so that doing this in several ways appropriate to diverse intentions, we may accomplish it. In what follows, a certain mode of doing this is proposed.

The First Practice, which is called
The Fixation of the Wheels

I

In order to prepare yourself for the exercise, it is first necessary to have a ready conception of the elements, that is to say, of those elements that can be explicated by things capable of becoming adjects, which can be produced by all actions and are most apt for the reception of all passions.

II

From these, then, are chosen thirty notations best suited for the expression of thirty letters; which provide the full number necessary to serve, in diverse ways, the pronunciation of three different languages. So that it will not be necessary to institute a threefold set of elements, let A be equivalent to α and א,[116] B similarly to β and ב,[117] and so on with the rest. Where the elements pass beyond our alphabet into Greek letters, such as ψ, ω, and θ, or beyond these to the Hebrew letters, they are written in their own proper characters. In this way one set of elements serves for these three languages and all those subaltern to them.

---

116. The Greek and Hebrew letters alpha and aleph, respectively.

117. The Greek and Hebrew letters beta and beth, respectively.

Figure 7.

III

Let thirty adjects, therefore, be chosen that present themselves to your imagination promptly, without any possibility of delay, when some other person or you yourself direct you to respond promptly with the individual elements in order, backwards or forwards, or out of order in whatever way may be desired.

IV

When this has been done, the next step is to assign each adject to its letter by appropriate operations, as though they were perceived by the eyes, and not without the appropriate bodily movement. You may order them and set them up in whatever way seems convenient to you. Below we present a set of images of this kind.[118]

---

118. All the following images are from Greek mythology, and most of them are taken directly from Ovid's *Metamorphoses*, a very popular work in Bruno's time. The modern student may find it more useful to use characters and activities from a more familiar source.

AGENTS AND ACTIONS

Lycas at the banquet	A A
Deucalion casting stones	B B
Apollo slaying Python	C C
Argus guarding the cow	D D
Arcas killing Callisto	E E
Cadmus sowing the dragon's teeth	F F
Semele giving birth	G G
Echo answering Narcissus	H H
A Tyrrhenian sailor worshipping Bacchus	I I
Pyramus stabbing himself	K K
Mineis spinning wool	L L
Perseus with Medusa's head	M M
Atlas holding up the sky	N N
Pluto seizing Proserpine	O O
Cyane dissolving in tears	P P
Arachne at the loom	Q Q
Neptune leading horses	R R
Pallas planting an olive tree	S S
Jason driving the bulls	T T
Medea brewing the bath for Æson	V V
Theseus making an image of gypsum	X X
Nisus' daughter cutting her father's hair	Y Y
Dædalus making wings	Z Z
Hercules wrestling with Antæus	Ψ Ψ
Orpheus playing the lyre	Φ Φ
The Ciconean women killing Orpheus	Ω Ω
Æsacus jumping from the cliff	Θ Θ
Memnon in his sepulchre	ע ע
Arion riding the dolphin	צ צ
Glaucus eating the herb	ש ש

In this it is not necessarily required for the first letter to be in the name of the agent or the action; it may be included in something of which it is expressive; it is enough that both should be connected in a determinate manner with that which signifies them.[119]

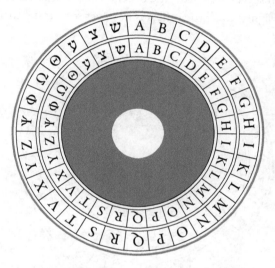

Figure 8. This is how at first one wheel should be situated inside the other, both being immobile; the outer wheel represents people, while the inner denotes the actions appropriate to them.

V

By what follows, progress is readily made to the final operation. Let us then agree to add, to the people and people's actions already described, such instruments or emblems as are not already included in the actions, but which can be adaptable or compatible with all things that proceed from the action. This is not done in such a way that the wheel should remain perpetually fixed in place, but that one appropriate adject to each figure should be fixed in our memories,

119. As noted in the introduction, As noted in the introduction, avoiding any obvious connection between the letters signified by the figure in the image, and the name of that figure, may have been intended for use in cryptography.

so that when they go this way and that way, they can always at once be referred to that (as will be revealed later on) to which the present things are ordained.

Let Lycas therefore have a chain, Deucalion a priest's fillet, Apollo an archer's belt, Argus a headstall, Arcas a bag, Cadmus a nosegay, Semele a chair to sit upon, and so on successively with the others. That each of these things should be able to be assigned to all the others is however something that must be pre-

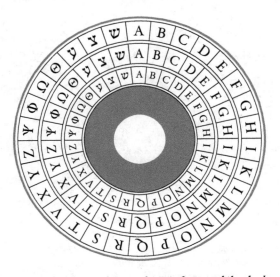

Figure 9. Here, at the second stage, the immobile wheel is within two other that are immobile, so that two things can be appropriated to it; which are referred to the people, for the sake of uniformity, by being collocated with them. Thus they are always able to present the nature of the elements wherever they are put, and in whatever way they are disposed. The fixed wheels are to be contemplated by the eye of the mind in this form.

served. The structure of the final practice and its completion will be revealed by the structure of the initial practice.

Here the outside wheel signifies people, the middle their proper actions, and the inner their insignia, in this way:

A	Lycas	A	At the banquet	A	In chains
B	Deucalion	B	With the stones	B	Wearing a fillet
C	Apollo	C	Slaying Python	C	Wearing a belt

| D | Argus | D | Watching the cow | D | With a headstall |
| E | Arcas | E | Hunting Callisto | E | Holding a bag[120] |

Proceed to institute, order, and judge the same way with the others. Whenever the signification of the third letter requires you to add an instrument (although if it would be inconvenient, because of an appropriate or contingent action, do not allow this to be placed in the figure's hand) for convenience, let it be imagined to be joined to some adject or linkage or interaction, so that the letter disturbs or helps the action, or is flung away, turned inside out, taken away, extracted, emptied, cast down, cut up, or something else that can be done to it congruent to the action. For the rest, it is incomparably more convenient to indicate things in this manner; indeed, such insignia should be able to refer and to be applied to all things.

VI

We have quite deliberately left to your own industry the finding of congruent actions and organs, without emblems, as indeed it happens that the peculiarities of any given person will be more noted and celebrated when taken one at a time; therefore (as each draws according to his pleasure) the persons have the instruments by which to labor and the insignia, the more to call forth and the more to incite the feelings. By this, they say, the gates of memory are affected, and the more powerfully, the wider they will open; for these things truly are not the same, nor do they emanate from the same things in all their principles.

On the Motion of the Wheels

I

Pressing on, therefore, from the aforesaid fixed wheels, which are held in the mind as long as it is convenient to keep them immobile, it is time for you to proceed to the more advanced practice, of which you will come first to the first composition, which is constituted of any two letters whatsoever. You have seen

---

120. This is oddly reminiscent of the 20th-century board game *Clue*—"Col. Mustard, in the library, with a pistol"—suggesting at least one modern source for imagery for a method like Bruno's.

the first figure consisting of two fixed wheels. Now leave the outer wheel fixed, while the inner is allowed to turn. Previously the fixation of what ought to be fixed as a habit was observed; now, so that its great and uncountably many operations ought to be innumerably multiple, it is able to revolve in both directions.

II

On the motion of the inner wheel of the first figure, to compose anything that may be represented by two letters

The operation just described gives what is proper to each thing. Now let anything that is communicable be offered to everything in the circle. Let whatever it may be consequently be adapted to the exigencies of composition of whatever is to be constituted. Lycaon at the banquet previously gave to you the twinned element AA, when the A of the inner wheel was beneath A of the outer wheel, and similarly Deucalion with the stones gave BB. Now, letting the wheels turn freely, you have images that are not twins but composed of two different letters. Say that the B of the smaller wheel is moved below the A of the greater wheel; then you no longer have AA, Lycaon at the feast, but Lycaon is changed so that he now throws stones. Deucalion killing Python, Apollo watching the cow, and so on successively, each one takes the operation of the next, receiving a new element from the figure succeeding it. How would you produce the combination PA? Put A of the inner wheel under P of the outer wheel, and they will present to you the image of Plato at the banquet.[121] The nature of the combination RE? Put E of the inner wheel under R of the outer wheel and they will be represented to you by Neptune stabbing Callisto. Similarly, the combination SI is represented by Pallas worshipping Bacchus, VO by Medea kidnapping Proserpine, and so on. In this way you have what you need to compose two letters to produce the meaning that is to be represented.

III

Of the motion of the inner wheels according to any figure and composition that may be represented by three letters

Likewise in the second figure, by allowing the two inner wheels to turn freely and easily compose any combination, you will be able to represent anything that

---

121. Earlier, Bruno assigned P to Cyane, not Plato.

has three letters. Whereas when the three wheels were fixed, Lycas at the banquet in chains presented to you AAA, now Lycas holding the head of Medusa with Pluto's emblem will give you AMO. Arcas acting like Semele with Pluto's emblem will give you EGO. Medea acting like the Tyrrhenian sailor with Perseus' emblem will give you VIM.[122] Thus, by changing the letters of the middle and inner wheel in many ways, under each letter of the outer wheel, anything that can be imagined that comes from the combination of three letters can be produced at will.

IV

On composing anything that can be represented by four letters, according to one method

If it happens that something needs to be composed from four letters, there is no need to suppose a fourth wheel, for not all letters happen to come fourth, but only a few certain ones take that place, as S in the combination MENS comes fourth, and T in the combination DANT[123] comes fourth.[124] For this purpose, therefore, something may be designated to represent the fourth letter, of which these are examples; it is sufficient to have something determined that happens to or appears with something that habitually occurs with the subject or adject to be imagined, which indicates the fourth letter by its presence; its absence will indicate otherwise.

V

On changing a composition that can be represented by three letters according to a different method

There is another way in which a fourth letter can be added onto a third. Let the letters L, R, and N standing and existing in the middle between letters, as in the first combination[125] of letters in the composition TRUNCUS, in the second of

---

122. These are the Latin words for "I love," "I," and "strength," respectively.

123. These are respectively the Latin words for "mind" and "they give."

124. Since word endings in Latin have grammatical meaning, that is, it is convenient to have emblems to represent common final letters. This will take care of many four-letter combinations.

125. By a combination Bruno means a syllable or other component part of a word—for example, the first combination mentioned in this sentence is TRUN, the second CRASS, and the

this composition INCRASSATUS, and in the third of this composition PER-MAGNUS.[126] To present these letters and denote their places, the others must have their modes or sensible accidents in the subject, or with the subject, or you must be able to direct them to the subject. To do this I usually put in a reasonable adject that signifies it, which is either seated in the third place, or resting on the second, or standing first. If other letters should offer themselves beyond this, as rarely happens in Latin, Greek, Hebrew, Aramaic, Persian, Italian, Arabic, and Spanish, we assist the first three elements according to the method you have already seen, while others are provided for in a different way.

What pertains to French (and this will also apply to German, Gothic, Scythian, and other languages of the same kind), which admit the inclusion of certain silent elements, not out of linguistic backwardness, but because of some habitual custom or other, this is not something with which you need to concern yourself, for they add nothing more to what is needed for complete writing. Thence they are not lacking, especially among those serious men of genius who seek to rescue their language from the harm caused by an apparent lack of cultivation.

VI

On composing anything that can be represent by five letters

For a composition of five letters, we do not need to add anything new, but we use (or, to speak more plainly) we combine what has already been proposed, since there is nothing that cannot be said using the two methods just mentioned in combination. Thus by adding S and T get four elements, and intermediate L, R, and N to get five, as in the combination PLEBS, the first combination in TRANSACTUM, and the last combination in STUPRANS.[127]

VII

On composing anything from many letters

For one or two particular words, however, which are not at all well known, what method are we to use when there are many letters compact together in a single

---

third GNUS. Latin lends itself to this sort of division.

126. These are respectively the Latin words for "trunk," "thickened," and "very great."

127. These are respectively the Latin words for "common people," "having been transacted," and "stupefying."

combination? This requires very little to be added to what we have already discussed, since a composition of four or five letters may easily be put together to represent it. I know that this is indeed the case with, among others, SCROBS,[128] which can be remembered easily by composing out of five letters SCROPS, on account of its similarity of sound.

VIII

On U after Q

Nor will I pass over in silence what should be noted in inner writing (even though it resides in the class of useful rather than of necessary things). The letter U after Q need not be counted, inasmuch as Q has the same effect without U as with it, and never appears without it. Plainly, then, QU has the power of a single letter; and thus, where the letter be present, as if one should write QUINTE QUARE QUADRUM QUINTUM QUATIS?[129] where indeed it would be necessary to use it; it would not be amiss to write "Qare qinte qatis qadrum qintum?"[130] This may be done habitually to silent letters without prejudice to the whole or the greater part of learning; for those who are studying foreign languages, it would appear to be the better option to include silent letters, which would be unnecessary in our own language.

IX

To amplify the inner field of subjects and most easily multiply the number of adjects, after it has become easy for you to work with a few adjects and a modest number of subjects

Concerning the multiplication of subjects I will add nothing, except what pertains to the qualities of what is to be multiplied. On this consideration I would say that some of them are more tenacious, and are accustomed to retain all adjects more easily. You will grasp this by probing the sources of effects and de-

---

128. In Latin, "ditch." Note that scrops can be spelled with the Greek letter Ψ, Psi, thus saving a letter; this is the point of Bruno's comment.

129. A deliberately silly Latin sentence meaning "Quintus, why do you strike the square for the fifth time?"

130. This is the same sentence; word order does not change meaning in Latin.

fects, according to the teaching expressed by us, and you may yourself compare the resemblance of others to them.

For the very extensive multiplication of adjects, on the other hand, after three days of practice, you will be able to provide yourself with a memorable beginning that will be of use to you for all purposes; having grasped one proportion, we may turn to all other similarly proportioned things that are to be learned.

You have had, alongside the number of letters, thirty most durable adjects, which were able to serve you for writing brief things. Now it helps immensely (provided that you do the work) to enlarge the page, to greatly multiply the number of adjects assigned to words; for it would indeed be inconvenient if a great many adjects of the same form were to appear over and over again, for variety is required in internal writing where it is not at all required for external writing, where it is enough simply to be well practiced in its exercise.

Well, then! Since you already have one each of Lycaon, Deucalion, etc., you may now shape yourself two Lycaons, Deucalions, and the rest, so that where you once had thirty, now you have sixty available to you. Triple them, and you will have ninety; quadruple them and you have one hundred twenty. So that your image strikes the imagination better, bring in thirty root names, all of which you know very well; this does not prohibit using the proper name of another. The name Philotheus, for example, will remain perpetually colored with the character of the name Deucalion once it has been numbered and written with the stones being thrown. Let it be remembered that this is better discovered by using and applying it to other things than you will be able to grasp by comprehending the surface alone.

On the Second Practice,
which is of simple terms representing any
composition formed of many letters together

I

It is indeed an important practice, preparing the way for the first mature practice, which in a certain place first sets out for you the combination of letters, in order to explicate whole words; so that each combination gives a composition. Thus to the number of subjects, you will be able to add perfect adjects (which are called uncombined and simple terms), and then accept numbers.

II

It does this in the following way. Just as with the thirty elements, you set up thirty active agents, emblems, circumstances, and things nearby, so now you arrange one hundred and fifty, which are made by placing each of the five vowels beside each of the letters in order. Thus in the same way that we have taught the combination of letters, we may be understood to teach of their combinations.

III

According what we have briefly said about enlarging the number of adjects, the most famous names are provided, seeing that to this necessary art, variety is most conducive, and you should bring certain principal and very notable names that are to be added, like bands of soldiers under the shadows and wings of your thirty banners. For the most ample operation, you will expand each of the banners already described by a set of five vowels, setting out another five banners.

IV

You should therefore note well that this number of banners is referred to, so that each obtains its place, by which their quality may be seen to come together. Where banners are concerned, indeed, the more a soldier becomes used to them, the more of them the armies may add, out of which one or two will be enough for the soldiers. It is by equality of proportions, not by precise equality of numbers, that all things are to be done.

V

You will therefore choose for yourself one hundred and fifty names, which are ordered either by their proper name, or by their customary action, or according to the order by which they are added to the list, and are informed by five letters. Once this is done, you should put in order the following list or another (if you have a better one) of parts and arts (so that they may be assigned to actions and describable arts), or of the names of notations you have made which follow in order from the place where they will be put; or any other way convenient to you, according to what is appropriate for us to put in order, using other things following in a definite place, so that it can be reduced to an uncertain series; so that by their relations, or by other circumstances, the same or other emblems and things can be added to them.

VI

You should next put these together in the image of the three previously mentioned wheels, five foxed wheels, of which each one is composed of one hundred fifty combinations of two elements.[131] Of these, the first and outermost will signify agents, under the names of inventors. The second wheel signifies actions. The third, emblems worn by the agents. The fourth, things standing next to the agents. The fifth, things around the agents. These latter are added to the agents, however, in such a way that each does not preserve its own; next to another image they carry the same meaning always.

---

131. As shown in the lists that follow, the thirty letters of Bruno's wheel are combined with the five vowels to yield 150 memory places. The lists are combined to transform Latin words into concise memory images.

Fig. 10. Since it is difficult to draw five wheels together on account of their width, we place one here as an image of the others, and that not extended but contracted. Thus the thirty primary banners are set in order around the circumference, and the five subordinates of each one are ordered in ladders from each one to the center.

INVENTORS

LETTERS		INVENTOR	INVENTION	No.
A	A	Rhegima	making bread from chestnuts	1
A	E	Osiris	farming	2
A	I	Ceres	yoking oxen	3
A	O	Triptolemus	sowing seed	4
A	U	Pitumnus	manuring fields	5
B	A	Erichthonius	wagons	6
B	E	Glaucus	hammering iron	7
B	I	Thraces	sickles	8
B	O	Misa	preserving with salt	9
B	U	Pyrodes	striking fire with flint	10
C	A	Hasamon	transplanting	11
C	E	Phega	grafting	12
C	I	Belhaiot	driving donkeys	13
C	O	Pilumnus	grinding grain	14
C	U	Oresteus	tending grapevines	15
D	A	Noah	making wine	16
D	E	Liber	making beer	17
D	I	Staphylus	getting raving drunk	18
D	O	Isis	laying out a garden	19
D	U	Minerva	olive oil	20
E	A	Aristeus	harvesting honey	21
E	E	Nimrod	hunting	22
E	I	Phalla	nets	23
E	O	Gebur	snares	24
E	U	Ramses	buckets	25

INVENTORS (cont.)

LETTERS		INVENTOR	INVENTION	No.
F	A	Regomer	ladders	26
F	E	Sargum	baskets	27
F	I	Danaus	digging wells	28
F	O	Doxius	building with mud bricks	28
F	U	Jubal	building with wood	30
G	A	Husbal	roasting lime	31
G	E	Cyclops	towers	32
G	I	Theodorus	lathes	33
G	O	Perdix	cooking	34
G	U	Talus	saws	35
H	A	Theodotus	gimlets	36
H	E	Parug	hammers	37
H	I	Semeol	wine-presses	38
H	O	Seusippus	trapping	39
H	U	Luscinus	axes	40
I[132]	A	Choræbus	pottery	41
I	E	Barcham	spinning wool	42
I	I	Closter	warping a loom	43
I	O	Arachne	weaving	44
I	U	Boetius	sewing	45
K	A	Phrigio	singing	46
K	E	Caathar	shoes	47
K	I	Procon	dyes from plants	48
K	O	Licarnassus	tongs	49
K	U	Chares	gloves	50

---

132. Published editions of Bruno routinely garble the letter pairs in these lists, leaving out the non-Latin letters. I have corrected the list to correspond to Bruno's 30-character alphabet.

INVENTORS (cont.)

LETTERS		INVENTOR	INVENTION	No.
L	A	Abas	shaving the head	51
L	E	Stram	razors	52
L	I	Crates	polishing gold	53
L	O	Arphalus	gilding	54
L	U	Dubitrides	storage pots	55
M	A	Hermahel	combs	56
M	E	Ramesses	tapestries	57
M	I	Minos	sailing	58
M	O	Dædalus	masts and rigging	59
M	U	Glycera	garlands	60
N	A	Emor	dancing	61
N	E	Anacharsis	using bellows	62
N	I	Delos	smelting brass	63
N	O	Lydius	coinage	64
N	U	Apis	doctoring	65
O	A	Chiron	surgery	66
O	E	Circe	witchcraft	67
O	I	Pharphacon	necromancy	68
O	O	Aiguam	magical circles	69
O	U	Hostanes	summoning demons	70
P	A	Zoroaster	magic	71
P	E	Suah	palmistry	72
P	I	Chaldæus	divination by fire	73
P	O	Attalus	divination by water	74
P	U	Prometheus	sacrificing oxen	75

INVENTORS (cont.)

LETTERS		INVENTOR	INVENTION	No.
Q	A	Abel	offering livestock	76
Q	E	Enoch	building an altar	77
Q	I	Zedechor	sacrifice into water	78
Q	O	Cureta	sacrificing children	79
Q	U	Abraham	circumcision	80
R	A	John	baptism	81
R	E	Emael	uncovering men's heads before the altar	82
R	I	Imus	veiling women's heads before the gods	83
R	O	Amphiaraus	augury	84
R	U	Orpheus	initiations	85
S	A	Aphares	Bacchic mysteries	86
S	E	Crithon	Eleusinian mysteries	87
S	I	Belus	idols	88
S	O	Diagoras	overturning altars	89
S	U	Chemis	burial in pyramids	90
T	A	Mirchanes	wax	91
T	E	Gyges	painting	92
T	I	Marsyas	playing the flute	93
T	O	Tubal	playing the lyre	94
T	U	Amphion	written music	95
V	A	Amurius	strings made of gut	96
V	E	Baros	strings made of brass	97
V	I	Venus	prostitution	98
V	O	Tubalcain	fighting	99
V	U	Pysaeus	bronze trumpets	100

INVENTORS (cont.)

LETTERS		INVENTOR	INVENTION	No.
X	A	Birrias	drum	101
X	E	Bellerophon	riding a horse	102
X	I	Neptune	taming horses	103
X	O	Ætholus	spears	104
X	U	Persæus	arrows	105
Y	A	Arthemon	fighting in formation	106
Y	E	Phœnix	crossbows	107
Y	I	Maletes	banners	108
Y	O	Gægar	shields	109
Y	U	Ermus	bells	110
Z	A	Marmitus	breastplates and helmets	111
Z	E	Thoth	writing in letters	112
Z	I	Conradus	writing contracts	113
Z	O	Thales	eclipses and the polar stars	114
Z	U	Pythagoras	morning and evening stars	115
Ψ	A	Nauphides	the course of the sun	116
Ψ	E	Endymion	the movements of the moon	117
Ψ	I	Hipparchus	precession of the equinoxes	118
Ψ	O	Atlas	the celestial sphere	119
Ψ	U	Archimedes	the atmosphere	120
Φ	A	Cleostratus	the twelve signs	121
Φ	E	Archita	the geometry of the cube	122
Φ	I	Xenophanes	innumerable worlds	123
Φ	O	Plato	the Ideas and what come from them	124
Φ	U	Raymundus	the nine elements	125

INVENTORS (cont.)

LETTERS		INVENTOR	INVENTION	No.
Ω	A	Ior.[133]	*Key* and *Shadows*	126
Ω	E	Protagoras	two contrary arguments	127
Ω	I	Alcmeon	the order of nature	128
Ω	O	Euclid	evil as nothingness	129
Ω	U	[omitted in text]		130
Θ	A	Epicurus	freedom of the soul	131
Θ	E	Timon	misanthropy	132
Θ	I	Crates	bread of the fountains	133
Θ	O	Cleanthes	completion of philosophy	134
Θ	U	Menedemus	prodigiously superstitious	135
‫ב‬	A	Polymnestus	the Pythagorean cult of beans	136
‫ב‬	E	Philolaus	the evident harmony of things	137
‫ב‬	I	Speusippus	pleasant philosophy	138
‫ב‬	O	Anaxagoras	chaos	139
‫ב‬	U	Archelaus	nature without balance	140
‫צ‬	A	Pyrrho	seeking and not finding	141
‫צ‬	E	Diodorus	complex and hard distinctions	142
‫צ‬	I	Simon	affirming everything by will	143
‫צ‬	O	Æschylus	masks	144
‫צ‬	U	Diogenes	the learned being ignorant of their own faults	145
‫ש‬	A	Homer	the Sophocles of epic poetry	146
‫ש‬	E	Sophocles	the Homer of tragedy	147
‫ש‬	I	Pharmacon	optics	148
‫ש‬	O	Tapes	perspective	149
‫ש‬	U	Melicus[134]	the art of memory	150

133. This is Bruno himself, under the Latin version of his name *Iordanus Brunus*, as inventor of the memory system taught in this book.

134. This is Simonides, the legendary founder of the Art of Memory.

ADJECTIVES

A	A	knotted[135]	1	F	A	fastidious	26
A	E	deceiving	2	F	E	uprooted	27
A	I	rolled up	3	F	I	fatal	28
A	O	formless	4	F	O	exempt	28
A	U	famous	5	F	U	out of breath	30
B	A	inert	6	G	A	brutal	31
B	E	unworthy	7	G	E	indisposed	32
B	I	dressed	8	G	I	hanging	33
B	O	inept	9	G	O	undigested	34
B	U	lying down	10	G	U	indiscreet	35
C	A	shod	11	H	A	wandering	36
C	E	unheard	12	H	E	destitute	37
C	I	inconstant	13	H	I	repulsed	38
C	O	disorderly	14	H	O	scrupulous	39
C	U	enchanted	15	H	U	ugly	40
D	A	approaching	16	I	A	supposititious	41
D	E	entrapped	17	I	E	buried	42
D	I	near	18	I	I	shaken	43
D	O	horrible	19	I	O	roaming	44
D	U	powerless	20	I	U	flowing	45
E	A	hitting	21	K	A	inclined	46
E	E	unhonored	22	K	E	harmful	47
E	I	festive	23	K	I	infused	48
E	O	carrying	24	K	O	renewed	49
E	U	expecting	25	K	U	unseen	50

---

135. This list is just as jumbled in the Latin original as it is in English translation.

ADJECTIVES (cont.)

L	A	discovered	51	Q	A	strict	76
L	E	obliged	52	Q	E	mysterious	77
L	I	put in the calendar	53	Q	I	portentous	78
L	O	bereaved	54	Q	O	ignoring[137]	79
L	U	piecemeal	55	Q	U	restful	80
M	A	broken	56	R	A	weeping	81
M	E	woven	57	R	E	aggressive	82
M	I	unusual	58	R	I	bereaved[138]	83
M	O	sprinkled	59	R	O	neglected	84
M	U	deceiving[136]	60	R	U	oppressed	85
N	A	leaning on	61	S	A	busy	86
N	E	ignoring	62	S	E	accursed	87
N	I	wounded	63	S	I	new	88
N	O	hurt	64	S	O	obscure	89
N	U	stupid	65	S	U	obscene	90
O	A	hungry	66	T	A	impenetrable	91
O	E	murmuring	67	T	E	drying	92
O	I	repeated	68	T	I	hard	93
O	O	impeded	69	T	O	dangerous	94
O	U	unrecountable	70	T	U	precipitous	95
P	A	unclean	71	V	A	venal	96
P	E	weak	72	V	E	stimulated	97
P	I	begging	73	V	I	pusillanimous	98
P	O	polymorphous	74	V	O	unbridled	99
P	U	obstructing	75	V	U	broken	100

---

136. The same word, *mentitum* in Latin, is already assigned to AE.

137. The same word, *ignoratum* in Latin, is already assigned to NE.

138. The same word, *orbatus* in Latin, is already assigned to LO.

Adjectives (cont.)

X	A	flagrant	101	Ω	A	formless[139]	126
X	E	gaping	102	Ω	E	dissonant	127
X	I	incised	103	Ω	I	deserted	128
X	O	twisted	104	Ω	O	forested	129
X	U	fuming	105	Ω	U	desirable	130
Y	A	shipwrecked	106	Θ	A	Stygian	131
Y	E	dyed	107	Θ	E	lacustrine	132
Y	I	chained	108	Θ	I	sleepy	133
Y	O	thin	109	Θ	O	young	134
Y	U	straying	110	Θ	U	ghostly	135
Z	A	frozen	111	ב	A	swelling	136
Z	E	full of holes	112	ב	E	armed	137
Z	I	funereal	113	ב	I	insipid	138
Z	O	bloodstained	114	ב	O	stony	139
Z	U	livid	115	ב	U	fierce	140
Ψ	A	putrid	116	צ	A	ambiguous	141
Ψ	E	pestiferous	117	צ	E	lascivious	142
Ψ	I	biting	118	צ	I	rabid	143
Ψ	O	drunken	119	צ	O	roaring	144
Ψ	U	troubled	120	צ	U	rapacious	145
Φ	A	oblique	121	ש	A	unspeakable	146
Φ	E	Tartarean	122	ש	E	discordant	147
Φ	I	shaking	123	ש	I	biting	148
Φ	O	forceful	124	ש	O	kicking	149
Φ	U	bitter	125	ש	U	stupified	150

---

139. The same word, *informe* in Latin, as assigned to AO.

OBJECTS

		SUITABLE FOR THE HEAD[140]				SUITABLE FOR THE HEAD (cont.)	
A	A	olive[141]	1	E	A	mane	21
A	E	laurel	2	E	E	hair	22
A	I	myrtle	3	E	I	iris	23
A	O	rosemary	4	E	O	Juno's crown[144]	24
A	U	cypress	5	E	U	raining clouds	25
B	A	palm	6	F	A	rising to a point	26
B	E	ivy	7	F	E	candles	27
B	I	poppy	8	F	I	Tisiphone's mane[145]	28
B	O	oak	9	F	O	gems	29
B	U	nettle	10	F	U	lilies	30
C	A	flowers	11	G	A	half moon	31
C	E	thorns	12	G	E	lightning	32
C	I	triple tiara[142]	13	G	I	sword	33
C	O	horn	14	G	O	axe	34
C	U	horns	15	G	U	arrow	35
D	A	royal crown	16	H	A	saw	36
D	E	morion[143]	17	H	E	rain	37
D	I	reeds	18	H	I	hook	38
D	O	willow	19	H	O	bridle	39
D	U	deer's antlers	20	H	U	vibrating tongue	40

140. The following objects, in other words, can be placed on the head of a memory image to add an additional syllable.

141. That is, a wreath made of olive leaves, which was used as a headdress in ancient times. The same is true of other plants mentioned in this list.

142. The traditional headdress of the Pope.

143. A helmet of the Renaissance era, most familiar nowadays as the usual helmet of Spanish conquistadors.

144. This traditionally had battlements, like the top of a medieval tower.

145. A mane of serpents, like that of Medusa.

OBJECTS (cont.)

SUITABLE FOR THE HEAD (cont.)				SUITABLE FOR THE NECK (cont.)			
I	A	cone	41	N	A	chain	61
I	E	grasping hand	42	N	E	ring	62
I	I	eagle's beak	43	N	I	ghost[147]	63
I	O	boar's head	44	N	O	wing	64
I	U	lion's head	45	N	U	bundles	65
K	A	rolling waves	46	O	A	noose	66
K	E	tombstone	47	O	E	quiver	67
K	I	wild owl	48	O	I	belt	68
K	O	chicken	49	O	O	sieve	69
K	U	dove	50	O	U	millstone	70
L	A	pussywillows	51	P	A	yoke	71
L	E	hydra	52	P	E	purse	72
L	I	flames	53	P	I	fan	73
L	O	wind	54	P	O	scepter	74
L	U	bird's nest	55	P	U	whip	75
SUITABLE FOR THE NECK[146]							
M	A	collar	56	Q	A	flagon	76
M	E	snake	57	Q	E	trumpet	77
M	I	lambskin	58	Q	I	sword	78
M	O	fox skin	59	Q	O	trophy	79
M	U	necklace	60	Q	U	spear	80

---

146. That is, objects that can be slung around the neck or from the shoulders of a memory image to add an additional syllable.

147. Latin *lemur*. Why Bruno thought it made sense to hang a ghost around someone's neck is unclear.

OBJECTS (cont.)

SUITABLE FOR THE NECK (cont.)

R	A	cowl	81
R	E	sail	82
R	I	golden belt	83
R	O	herbs	84
R	U	pocket watch	85

SUITABLE FOR THE FEET[148]

S	A	scorpion	86
S	E	dog	87
S	I	cave	88
S	O	goose	89
S	U	altar	90
T	A	arbor	91
T	E	golden apple	92
T	I	snake	93
T	O	fetters	94
T	U	conch shell	95
U	A	column	96
U	E	dolphin	97
U	I	dragon	98
U	O	horse	99
U	U	wheel of fortune	100
X	A	hay	101
X	E	ditch	102
X	I	furnace	103
X	O	granary	104
X	U	cradle	105

SUITABLE FOR THE FEET (cont.)

Y	A	Hell	106
Y	E	lake	107
Y	I	lion	108
Y	O	rabbit	109
Y	U	path	110
Z	A	grove	111
Z	E	river	112
Z	I	piece of marble	113
Z	O	sow nursing piglets	114
Z	U	precipice	115
Ψ	A	throne	116
Ψ	E	chair	117
Y	I	tomb	118
Ψ	O	reflecting mirror	119
Ψ	U	entrails for divining	120
Φ	A	bull in the way	121
Φ	E	hollow full of honey	122
Φ	I	scarecrow	123
Φ	O	mousetrap	124
Φ	U	bundles of reeds	125
Ω	A	dead horse	126
Ω	E	sevenfold candelabra	127
Ω	I	smoking censer	128
Ω	O	burning sulphur	129
Ω	U	beam in the way	130

---

148. That is, objects that can be placed near the feet of a memory image to add another syllable.

OBJECTS (cont.)

SUITABLE FOR THE FEET (cont.)				SUITABLE FOR THE FEET (cont.)			
Θ	A	slow donkey	131	צ	A	furnace[152]	141
Θ	E	winecup	132	צ	E	smoldering tow	142
Θ	I	Pandora's vase[149]	133	צ	I	fishing shack	143
Θ	O	cornucopia	134	צ	O	bitch nursing puppies	144
Θ	U	hesitant bull	135	צ	U	chariot	145
ר	A	human trunk[150]	136	ש	A	rooster treading hen	146
ר	E	hanged woman	137	ש	E	ram charging	147
ר	I	wolf gnawing corpse	138	ש	I	pig digging	148
ר	O	hen sitting on eggs	139	ש	O	boy playing	149
ר	U	tomb[151]	140	ש	U	drum	150

---

149. In the oldest version of the Pandora legend, the container given to her by the gods was a vase, not a box.

150. That is, a corpse with its head and limbs hacked off. This and the next two are reminders of the pervasive violence of the world in which Bruno lived.

151. The same word, *sepulchrum* in Latin, already assigned to ΥI.

152. The same word, *fornax* in Latin, is already assigned to XI.

Magical Images

Images of the Faces of the Signs from Teucer the Babylonian, which may be drawn upon for the use and convenience of the present art

Aries

A A   There ascends in the first face of Aries a black man of vast stature, his eyes blazing and his face severe, with a white cloak wrapped about him.

A E   In the second, a not uncomely woman, dressed in a white tunic and a mantle dyed Tyrian purple over it, her hair unbound and crowned with laurel.

A I   In the third, a pale man with red hair, dressed in red clothing, carrying a golden bracelet in his left hand and an oaken rod in his right, unquiet and with an angry face, as though desiring things he cannot get and deeds he cannot do.

Taurus

A O   In the first face of Taurus, a naked man plowing, holding a dark-colored hat woven of straw, and after him another rustic lying with a woman.

A U   In the second, a naked man carrying a club, crowned, with a golden belt around his shoulders and a scepter in his left hand.

B A In the third, a man holding a snake in his left hand and a spear or arrow in his right, and before him a pot of fire and a jug of water.

Gemini

B E In the first face of Gemini, a man dressed as a servant, having a rod in his right hand, his face cheerful and jocund.

B I In the second, a man digging and laboring in the earth, and next to him a dancing flute player with bare feet and head.

B O In the third, a Moon holding a flute in his right hand and a sparrow in his left, and next to him an angry man seizing a stick.

Cancer

B U In the first face of Cancer, a woman crowned and richly dressed, holding an olive wreath in her right hand and a bowl in her left.

C A In the second, a man and a woman sitting at table, and they are dressed in the kind of clothes worn by those who play before wine is drunk;[153] before the woman are vessels of gold and silver.

C E In the third, a huntsman with dogs running before and after him, and he carries a horn and a crossbow, hurrying and wandering around without cease.

---

153. That is, dressed as minstrels.

Leo

C I In the first face of Leo, a red man dressed in yellow clothes and crowned in gold, carrying a rooster in his right hand, and riding a lion.

C O In the second, a woman walking in the sky with her hands outstretched, and next to her a man who appears ready to take revenge, having a drawn sword and a shield.

C U In the third, a man holding a bag or whip, with a sad, downcast, and unlovely face, who is followed by a youth dressed in white.

Virgo

D A In the first face of Virgo, a girl wearing a garland of flowers, and a man strewing flowers and leaves toward her, wearing garments of green that are unfastened.

D E In the second, a black man dressed in leather, holding a bag in his hand, having a cloak wrapped loosely about his head.

D I In the third, and old man leaning on two sticks, with dissheveled hair before his face, his beard unkempt, dressed in dark colors.

Libra

D O The first face of Libra has a man inspecting a balance, having a dagger or stylus in his right hand and a fierce expression on his face.

D U The second, two fighters and rioters before one who is seated at a tribunal, who has a rod extended in his right hand, and his left hand upraised.

Figure 11. Magical Image E A · Third Face of Libra

E A   The third, a fierce centaur, who is followed by a man holding bread and a goblet of wine, and preceded by a completely naked man.

Scorpio

E E   There ascends in the first face of Scorpio a woman who is lovely and well dressed, and two youths who have become angry at each other because of her, and fall to blows with each other until they are exhausted.

E I   In the second, a woman completely naked, and two wholly naked men, of whom one stands at the side of the woman, while the other lies on the ground, playing with a dog.

E O   In the third, a man exposing his back to be beaten by a woman, and holding his feet in his hands.

Sagittarius

E U   The first face of Sagittarius has a man in a full suit of armor, holding a round shield in his left hand, and in his right a very wide sword, in which the earth is seen to shake incessantly.

F A   The second, a sad woman dressed in mourning clothes, by turns holding a child in her arms and leading it by the hand.

F E   The third, a man lying on the ground and shaking a stick, his face pale and his clothes dirty, and a pig standing next to him, digging handfuls of earth.

Capricorn

F I   The first face of Capricorn, a man dressed as a merchant, his face ugly and sad, followed by a youth who dances and claps his hands.

Figure 12. Magical Image E U · First Face of Sagittarius

F O   The second, a man throwing a javelin at a flying dove, and two women, one of them embracing the man.

F U   The third, a virgin dressed in white, trampling a fox with her feet, and reading from a book.

Aquarius

G A   The first face of Aquarius has the father and mother of a family in the midst of thinking; he has pebbles in his hand, and she has a sieve.

G E   The second, a man in the dress of a counsellor, sitting with memoranda in his hands, and with a full beard hanging from his chin; his face appears very severe.

G I   The third, an angry youth whose face appears inflamed with rage, his hands as though attacking, and his fingers contorted.

Pisces

G O   In the first face of Pisces, the figure of a man carrying his possessions and looking for a new dwelling, followed by a woman carrying a tripod and a pole.

G U   In the second, a man girded as though for labor, with his clothes tied back and his arms bare to give his body agility, and a happy face.

H A   In the third, an adolescent in love embracing a girl, and next to them two peacocks contending with each other.

Although the habit and activity of the foregoing images are not conferred by the Art of Memory as such, they may however complete the logic of the images.

I.

The first image of Aries is bold, shameless, and strongly imaginative.

The second is prouder, ambitious, and magnanimous.

Figure 13. Magical Image G E · Second Face of Aquarius

The third is troubled and almost desperate, more acute of wit, and expects joy.

II.

The first image of Taurus supports the works and principal arts of geometry.

The second is powerful and noble among multitudes of peoples.

The third is needy, miserable, and servile.

III.

The first image of Gemini is learned in mathematics, without which no other faculty is useful.

The second is impudent, deceptive, and delights in labor, but bears no fruits.

The third is delirious, forgetful, and very talkative.

IV.

The first image of Cancer is of subtle contemplation, attentive mind, and a will prone to love.

The second, a moderate wit but a great fortune.

The third, of much business and modest following through, on account of the difficulty of means.

V.

The first image of Leo is impetuous, luxurious, severe, and implacable.

The second, quick to shed blood, treacherous and suspicious.

The third is companionable and friendly, and would rather lose a fight than persevere in it.

VI.

The first image of Virgo accumulates riches, but not by illicit business.

The second avidly and intently takes pains to increase things.

The third debilitates, weakens, terminates, and consumes.

VII.

The first image of Libra is just, rescuing the poor from the hands of the powerful and violent.

The second is impatient of iniquity and pacifies tumults.

The third is a fornicator, adulteress, and devourer.

VIII.

The first image of Scorpio is a lovely and sweet betrayer and evildoer.

The second is as faithless as it is ugly.

The third is openly angry, full of indignation, and violent.

IX.

The first image of Sagittarius is bold and furious, and detests the yoke of every law.

The second conceives sorrow from fear and gives birth to obsequiousness.

The third has long hair, and is quarrelsome and an enemy of peace.

X.

The first image of Capricorn loses its substance through extravagance.

The second seeks impossible things.

The third is very intent on increasing things, but is deceived where wisdom is concerned.

XI.

The first image of Aquarius cogitates and labors to make money, but is pressed by poverty and vileness.

The second has much intelligence and sobriety.

The third has immoderate impudence and presumption.

XII.

The first image of Pisces is troubled by material poverty.

The second is intent on many and great business affairs.

The third drowses in much leisure and luxury.

It is permissible not to apply these to work with the images, but they are necessary to the forms and qualities of the images. They truly depict the sense and species of the images.

Here follow
Seven images of Saturn
from the Egyptian and Persian philosophers,
which can be put to use as places and subjects.

H E   The first image of Saturn. A man with a stag's head, riding a dragon, having in his right hand an owl that is devouring a serpent.

H I   The second is a man holding a sickle in his right hand and a fish in his left, riding a camel.

H O   The third is a sorrowful and lamenting man, dressed in dark clothing, with his hands raised toward heaven.

H U   The fourth is a black man with camel's feet, seated on a flying dragon, bearing branches of cypress in his right hand.

I A   The fifth, a man dressed in black clothing and with a black face, with a basilisk in his right hand, its tail wrapping around his arm.

I E   The sixth, an old lame man leaning on a staff, seated on a high throne placed on a chariot, which is drawn by a mule and a donkey.

I I   The seventh, a charioteer in a chariot drawn by two stags, holding a fish in one hand and a curved sickle in the other.

Seven images of Jupiter

I O   The first image of Jupiter, a handsome man in a chariot drawn by dragons, throwing an arrow with his right hand at one dragon's head.

I U   The second image of Jupiter, a man seated on a throne which is carried through the air by four winged youths, who carry branches of the beech tree.

Figure 14. Magical Image I U · Second Image of Jupiter

K A The third is a man with a ram's head, seated on a wheel, and carrying a vessel of balsam in his hand.

K E The fourth is a man who has a lion's head and the feet of an eagle, and holds an oak branch in his right hand, before whom bow two beautiful youths dressed in white.

K I The fifth is a man whose clothing is adorned with emeralds, seated on an eagle, wearing a crown of hyacinths and with a scepter in his hand.

K O The sixth is a crowned man dressed in yellow clothes, holding an olive branch in his right hand, and riding on a dragon.

K U The seventh is a crowned man with his hands upraised and joined, as though praying, whose clothing of sky blue is sprinkled with golden stars.

Seven images of Mars

L A The first image of Mars is a man in armor riding a lion, with a vulture pecking at his helmet with its beak. He is a man of savage appearance.

L E The second is an armored man with a broadsword and a spear, and on his helmet is something similar to a chimera, which vomits flames and sparks from its mouth.

L I The third is a man who casts burning sulfur from his right hand, the left having hold of the neck of a panther, whom he rides without its consent.

L O The fourth is a man who holds a sheathed sword and a human head dripping with blood in his right hand, and whose left hand appears to burn like the sun.

Figure 15. Magical Image K E · Fourth Image of Jupiter

L U   The fifth is a man of tawny color, dressed in red clothes, holding a heavy iron scepter and riding a wolf.

M A   The sixth is a man who ravishes a beautiful virgin by force, while she turns away from him. They are both in an ivory chariot drawn by two baboons.

M E   The seventh is a leopard and a tiger fighting, and on either side of them a shield menaced by a drawn sword.

Seven images of the Sun

M I   The first image of the Sun is a lovely crowned woman in a chariot of gold, drawn upwards by four horses.

M O   The second, a very beautiful youth, naked and crowned, who has many flowers entwined in his hair, and holds a peacock in his arms.

M U   The third, a diademed youth from whose head light shines in rays, holding a quiver and a bow.

N A   The fourth, a woman embracing and kissing a boy who is dressed in a green tunic, has tawny hair and a handsome face, and holds a mirror in his right hand.

N E   The fifth, a virgin seated upon a crocodile, holding a round shield in her left hand and throwing a dart with her right.

N I   The sixth, a man holding a rooster in his right hand, and riding a lion, who is running and breathing clouds of mist out of its nostrils.

N O   The seventh, a man dressed as a pope, who has a crow in his lap and a golden dog beneath his feet; two men with bare heads, clad in dark or tawny garments, come before him.

Figure 16. Magical Image M O · Second Image of the Sun

Seven images of Venus

N U The first image of Venus is a naked girl crowned with myrtle, with abundant hair reaching down to her heels, and holding a white puppy before her.

O A The second, a beautiful boy carrying a basket full of flowers in both hands, and followed by a man in the clothing of a gardener.

O E The third, the statue of a naked woman, who appears to have the head of a dove and the feet of an eagle; a youth follows her, and a man flees before her.

O I The fourth, a woman riding a bull, combing her hair with her right hand and holding a mirror in her left; by her stands a younger woman with a green bird in her hand.

O O The fifth, a boy wearing a silver chain, and next to him a naked girl, crowned like Bacchus with laurel, and dancing.

O U The sixth, a winged boy with hair that gleams like gold, whose wings have a thousand colors, casting a flaming javelin.

P A The seventh, a youth and a girl wrestling, both naked, and striving to conquer one another for this reason, that she has a golden chain in her hand.

Seven images portraying Mercury

P E The first image signifying and ordained for Mercury is a very beautiful youth with a scepter, about which two serpents entwine, facing one another over the upper end.

*Figure 17. **Magical Image N E · Fifth Image of the Sun***

P I   The second, a bearded and attractive youth, crowned with olive leaves, having a scepter in his hand, and before him a rising flame.

P O   The third, one having a winged helmet and heels, holding a rod in his left hand and a dart in his right.[154]

P U   The fourth image, a man with a beard hanging down over his chest, wearing a toga, who is followed by a girl with a sweet face and an altogether lovely body, but having a serpent's tail.

Q A   The fifth, slaying Argus,[155] having a spear in his right hand and shepherd's pipes in his left, and next to him a calf feeding on green herbs.

Q E   The sixth, a man dressed as a merchant and traveler, having his eyes turned toward the Sun, and his hands stretched out.

Q I   The seventh, a boy riding on a ram, holding its horn with his left hand, and a parrot in his right.

Seven images of the Moon

Q O   The first image of the Moon is a horned woman riding on a dolphin, having a chameleon in her right hand and a lily in her left.

Q U   The second, a rustic man in a hood, having a fish hook in his right hand, and supported by a three-pronged spear, which he holds with his left.

R A   The third, a woman adorned with many pearls, dressed in white garments, having a crystal vase in her right hand and a cat in her left.

R E   The fourth is a woman seated on a hydra with three necks, from each of which spring seven heads, and holding out her hands empty before her.

R I   The fifth, a boy with a silver crown and scepter, mounted on a chariot drawn by two goats.

154. That is, a conventional image of Mercury portrayed in this way.

155. Another conventional image of Mercury, who was said in myth to have slain the many-eyed Titan Argus.

Figure 18. **Magical Image P U · Fourth Image of Mercury**

R O   The sixth, a woman with a single horn, with her arms and legs entwined by serpents, riding on a panther.

R U   The seventh, a man dressed in linen clothes, setting a dog upon a wild boar.

An Image of the Lunar Dragon[156]

S A   A kingly man who has a dragon in his right hand; a flame of fire is above the head of the king, and the head of the dragon is similarly adorned.

Images of the 28 Mansions of the Moon
drawn for use in this Art[157]

S E   First, on an iron throne, an Ethiopian man throwing a dart, and girt about with a dark garment.

S I   Second, a king on a throne; with his scepter, he raises men who are fallen prostrate to the ground.

S O   Third, a woman very finely dressed and seated on a throne, her right hand raised above her head; on her left side is a foolish and fleeing woman covered in her own hair.

S U   Fourth, a knight seated on a horse, holding a serpent in his right hand and leading a black dog with his left.

T A   Fifth, a prince on a silver throne, his right hand holding a staff, his left embracing a girl.

T E   Sixth, two armored men uncover their heads, cast away their swords, and embrace each other.

T I   Seventh, a man who is praying and raises both hands toward heaven; he is well dressed and seated on a silver chair.

---

156. Lunar dragon: the lunar nodes, the points where the Moon's orbit crosses that of the sun, were pictured as the head and tail of a dragon.

157. The mansions of the Moon are divisions of the sky corresponding to the Moon's position on each of the 28 days of a lunar month, used in Arabic and Hindu astrology. Renaissance magic included magical workings and talismans drawing on the power of the Mansions, so it is not surprising to find Bruno using them as well.

Figure 19. Magical Image X A · 15ᵗʰ Mansion of the Moon

T O	Eighth, a man riding an eagle, holding a palm leaf in his right hand, and followed by two captives.
T U	Ninth, a eunuch covering his eyes with his hands, standing before a soiled bed.
U A	Tenth, a woman giving birth, and in front of her, a golden lion and a man who appears to be ill.
U E	Eleventh, a man riding a lion, holding its mane with his left hand and a spear with his right.
U I	Twelfth, in a dark and gloomy place, a dragon fighting a man.
U O	Thirteenth, a stallion mounting a mare, and a shepherd standing on his hands, supported by a staff, his face expressionless.
U U	Fourteenth, a man holding a dog suspended by its tail, and the dog thus held bites at its own paws.
X A	Fifteenth, a man sitting and reading letters, praising the one who delivered them.
X E	Sixteenth, a merchant weighing silver with a scale he holds in his hand, and another counting the coins.
X I	Seventeenth, a man carrying a chest, and followed by an ape.
X O	Eighteenth, a man with a copper serpent in his hand, and many serpents fleeing from him.
X U	Nineteenth, a woman waiting with her hand held over her face.
Y A	Twentieth, a centaur hunting, wearing a quiver and carrying a bow in his left hand, and in his right hand a dead fox.
Y E	Twenty-first, two men, one of them facing backwards and the other forwards, and between them a pile of their shaved hair.
Y I	Twenty-second, a man with a helmet and winged feet, fleeing to a place of safety.
Y O	Twenty-third, a cat with a dog's head, or a dog with a cat's body, digging in the ground, and a man falling to the ground.
Y U	Twenty-fourth, a woman nursing a child, and holding by one horn a ram, who is followed by a great flock.
Z A	Twenty-fifth, one planting a fig tree, and another sowing grain.

Figure 20. Magical Image Y I · 22ⁿᵈ Mansion of the Moon

Z E   Twenty-sixth, a woman washing and combing her hair, and before her a winged boy.

Z I   Twenty-seventh, a winged man dipping an empty and perforated jug in a well.

Z O   Twenty-eighth, a bronze fish cast into water, and many live ones gathering around it.

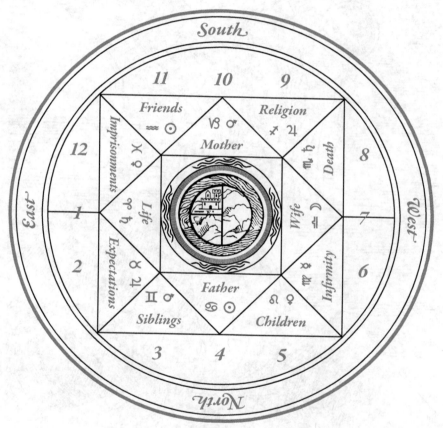

Fig. 21. The Twelve Houses of the Circle of the Heavens

Images of the Houses

Z U   The first image of the first house, a man sitting on his fundament, and another driving one sheep away from him and another toward him with a stick, near a bubbling fountain.

*Figure 22. **Magical Image ♀ A · Third Image of the Ninth House***

Ψ A　　The second image, a man sitting at a table, and his wife giving birth, and two midwives with her.

Ψ E　　The third image, a naked woman turning a wheel, with a cloth over her eyes, standing on a globe under which flowing waters are agitated.[158]

Ψ I　　The first image of the second house, two servants carrying vessels full of silver, jewels, and gold.

Ψ O　　The second, a man digging for treasure, and a naked old woman of surpassing leanness fleeing from him.

Ψ U　　The third, a man like a blacksmith, black-skinned and with curled hair, leaning on his work, and by him a little black boy, well dressed, with a golden crown in his hands.

Φ A　　The first image of the third house, like an image of Castor and Pollux standing above an altar, and between them a burning flame.

Φ E　　The second, one as though leaving his family and going away from a good place, his face sad and taciturn.

Φ I　　The third, like a hermit wrapped in a cowl, with a book in his hand, followed by an image of an angry Mars.

Φ O　　The first image of the fourth house, an old man with his aged wife buried in the midst of human bones, stretched out upon gold.

Φ U　　The second, a pretty woman having a globe of the Earth in her left hand, a crown in the shape of a tower on her head, and in her right hand a scepter, with which she seems to want to dig.

Ω A　　The third, a man standing by a grave surrounded by an iron railing, and with him a cow eating hay.

Ω E　　The first image of the fifth house, an elderly man with a full beard accompanied by two children, giving gifts to his friends, two of whom follow him smiling.

Ω I　　The second, a man with his eyes focused on a balance, and a messenger dressed in white and with a green cap approaching him.

---

158. This is closely based on the traditional Renaissance image of Fortune.

Figure 23. Magical Image ♋ U · First Image of the Eleventh House

Ω O   The third, a man with his wife or another woman, sitting at table, kissing and drinking.

Ω U   The first image of the sixth house, a sick man lying on the ground, and a lean and dark dog standing near him and stealing something from him.

Θ A   The second, a girl dressed as a queen, with a Moorish boy holding up the hem of her garment, and two dancing servant girls going before her with garlands in their hands.

Θ E   The third, a man with an orb in his left hand and a drawn sword in his right, and another man going before him.

Θ I   The first image of the seventh house, two men quarreling and putting their hands on the hilts of their swords, and between them a youth reading letters.

Θ O   The second, a handsome youth, and a virgin crowned with flowers, who is being embraced by an older man as they kiss each other.

Θ U   The third, a man in armor, who is followed by one who looks like a thief carrying away merchandise.

ע A   The first image of the eight house, a bare-chested man striking a stone, and with him a furious man shattering earthen vessels and spilling oil on the earth.

ע E   The second, one like Sisyphus who strains to roll a huge stone up a mountain, followed by a woman with her head and face veiled, and wearing a dark cloak.

ע I   The third, a rustic carrying fruit, and pulling after him a fox bound by a chain.

ע O   The first image of the ninth house. A very lovely woman dressed in green clothing, crowned with gold, having her right hand extended to the sky, and lightning descending before her.

ע U   The second, a man bowing and praying with his hands joined and raised above his head, and before him an altar on which a sacrifice is being consumed by fire.

ש A   The third is a virgin having a celestial globe in her left hand and a mirror in her right, dressed in celestial colors, and having a crown and shoes of shining gold.

ש E   The first image of the tenth house. A king sitting on his throne, with the men of his council sitting together before him, and several people bowing before them.

ש I   The second, a pious man seated in a bishop's chair, who holds up the image of a woman playing a trumpet.

ש O   The third, a copper column on which is the image of a naked king made of gold, and before it a priest who extends his two hands toward it.

ש U   The first image of the eleventh house. A beautiful naked woman with her head adorned with gems and gold, a necklace of shining rubies and pearls around her neck, and carrying a quiver and bow of gold.

ת A   The second, a host of servants carrying treasure.

ת E   The third, an old king walking in royal garments, followed by a boy in a dark garment that falls to his ankles, bareheaded, and carrying a royal crown in his hands.

ת I   The first image of the twelfth house, a man who greets a friend with one hand, and holds a knife hidden in the other, and between them a calf sleeping by a fire.

ת O   The second has grazing cattle, and next to them a yoke and a pack-saddle.

ת U   The third, a bare-chested man striking a stone, and with him a furious man shattering earthen vessels and spilling oil on the earth.

✛

The Use of the Images

The Practical Use of the Foregoing Images in Remembering Things

 ROM THAT WHICH has just been shown, you will be able to derive immense usefulness and incomparable convenience:

1. The forms themselves are always available as enduring subjects.

2. Subjects are arranged in this order, or can be put in this order, which is very conducive to holding the forms in memory.

3. If you want to convert these adjects into subjects and vice versa, what can stop you?

4. These permit the parts of things that are to be held in memory, as vivid images and symbols, to be combined in an orderly way with appropriate actions. Thus each of them, by acting, suffering, altering, changing position, and so on and so forth, in ways appropriate to them, having the proper modes by which they act, or by and around which other things act on them, they can describe material to be remembered in symbols that are divided among the parts of their bodies.

In all this, however, you should not neglect this point, that you ought never to choose forms that are at all abstract, but definite images that draw on the imaginative faculty of vision. I have explained elsewhere how we ought to make images so that they stir the outward senses, and thus potentially insinuate themselves into the inward senses.

On Combinations in which Letters
Subsisting Precede Letters Assisting

When things are disposed in this way, by infinite combinations out of a multitude of constituent letters, it is not necessary to add new orders to the primary composition. Since you have a hundred and fifty simple combinations in which the letters that assist, or are placed to assist, come before the letters that subsist, or are placed to subsist.[159] Thereby you may easily have a hundred fifty others, in which the letter that assists or is placed to assist comes after the letter that subsists or is placed to subsist. By such differences as straight or bent, clothed or naked, turned this way or that, sitting or standing, or a thousand others, you may duplicate your images so that they will accommodate you in this way. Thus Choræbus the potter sitting denotes *AM*, while standing he signifies *MA*.

Figure 24.

---

159. This is a complicated way of saying something simple. Bruno uses the verbs *adsistere* and *subsistere* (which I translate "assist" and "subsist") to remind the reader of the distinction, earlier in the book, between subjects and adjects. In this context, though, letters that subsist are the five vowels, and those that assist are the consonants.

Of Liquid and Final Letters Between and After the Simple Combinations

To add letters in the middle of a word, or onto the end without making use of the five combinations, my friend, you will by study be able to provide yourself amply using the methods we have shown for making combinations out of the basic set of five vowels. You will therefore choose eleven actions to signify the eleven final letters *C, D, G, L, M, N, P, R, S, T*, and *X*, and three others by which to show the medial liquids *L, N*, and *R*.[160] You can apply them first to the head of the figure and then to the back, or vice versa. In the same way you can assign eleven other actions to signify the final letters, and three for the medial letters, of which the first will be in the material that is subject to the action, and the second in the arm or the hand of the person carrying out the action. Similarly you can distinguish eleven and three circumstances. You will be able to apply these as adjects, and in practice you will apply them differently even though they are all of the same kind. This much we have communicated in a casual manner, so that the little that we have left out can be discovered by your own efforts.

Of Two Excellent Discoveries in this Art, and in Praise of Them

There are two things that we have discovered and perfected in this art, both of which were seen by all the ancients as impossible. The first relates to the first practice, by which we may distribute the combinations, as many as you please and of whatever kind you wish, to each subject. The second relates to the second practice (which is a discovery nearly divine, and pregnant with other discoveries, one of which is that anyone will know how to apply it), by which we can easily add to each subject and individual item in this art whatever ending is referred to it.[161]

Therefore our discovery permits internal writing to be done quickly and easily, and the fruits thereof will ripen through practice. As bleating letters must

---

160. All Latin words end either with a vowel or with one of the eleven consonants listed, and the three medial liquids are the only consonants that break Latin's otherwise rigid alternation of consonants and vowels. Other languages will of course require different arrangements.

161. Latin grammar is expressed largely by variations in word endings, and Bruno points out here that any word or object to be memorized can be supplied with the right grammatical ending by means of his method.

be driven together into syllables before they can be herded together, so we must learn to gather terms together into an oration. My curriculum for training in this art focuses on the first and second practices, so that while you are reading or listening, it can be applied to each subject in the order to which the latter is referred. Thereafter, when you use it, each of these things will appear promptly and, indeed, instantly. Therefore this art replaces every other art of this kind that has preceded it, nor need it fear being replaced by those that come after it. We believe that we have brought this thing to its summit; while other arts busy themselves with a hunt for letters or, more properly, a wild goose chase after them, we proceed term by term to the end of sermons and orations.

Of Practice with Things that Signify by Simple Terms

Next we proceed to the practice by which appropriate things are remembered. Things that are complex are to be signified by simple things. Those that can be grasped in their complex form are either substances or accidents.[162] Those that are substances are either sensible or intelligible.[163] Those that are sensible are either sensible per se, or by their accidents. Of those things that are accidents, some are in substances, such as quantity and intrinsic quality, while others inhere in substances as extrinsic qualities, such as colors and surrounding figures.

Some things are indeed in substances in one sense, and added to them in another; for example, habits, of which some have to do with what is, and others with what is said. Some exist in substances, such as those who act on patients and are acted on by agents. Some surround substances, and of these some surround because they have had substances added to them, and others because they have been added to substances, as extrinsic things are said to have done to them; others are conjoined to subjects by adjectives, as when something is said to be "wearing a ring," "wearing greaves," "clothed," or "married;"[164] others are adjuncts to a substance, such as "home," "prize," "wife."[165]

---

162. "Substance" and "accident," as noted earlier, are basic terms in Renaissance philosophy. This entire section is full of technical philosophical jargon.

163. Another standard distinction in Renaissance philosopy; "sensible" means experienced by the senses, "intelligible" means experienced by the mind.

164. All four of these are single words in Latin. Greaves are armor for the shins.

165. An adjunct is a substance that implies the existence of another substance: thus a home implies someone whose home it is, a prize implies a victor who wins it, and a wife implies a husband.

Some things are in substances in a certain sense and around them in another sense, as when something may be taken both as applying to all things in general and as a thing in itself, in its own individuality, as are time and space. Time is a single subject in the heavens and many subjects in each of those things that are said to exist in time.

Space is likewise one thing if we speak of it according to logical philosophy, in which it is that which surrounds all bounded things. According to common speech, a body is bounded by whatever surrounds it; according to most physicists, we call this space, the most definite dimension of matter and the container of all dimensions. Space is therefore in things and around things according to its mode, as will be obvious upon consideration.

Of all things that strike the memory forcefully, we must put figuration[166] first. Therefore simple intelligible subjects are represented by the images of sensible subjects, that they may become like the wheels and flames of Ezekiel.[167] Simple sensible substances are figured according to their accidents, disposed according to the upright forms of human beings, and the many forms of beasts that go with their bellies toward the ground.

Things that are sensible by means of their accidents are figured by those things that are objects to the senses as such. Accidents that are in substances are figured by those things they are in, as a certain quantity may be figured by something that has that continuous or discrete quantity.[168]

Quality as such is figured by something which has it as a property. Substances are figured by the accidents by which they are predisposed to be shaped. Accidents that inhere, by those things in which they are inherent; accidents that are added, by those things to which they are added; accidents that consist, by those things in turn of which they consist. Circumstantial accidents, which cannot be figured by themselves, are figured by those things of which they are circumstances or around which they are placed. These can be made into figures in turn by means of those figures by which they are brought before the senses.

---

166. That is, the process of creating figures or images.

167. The first chapter of the *Book of Ezekiel* contains vivid descriptions of angels having forms such as wheels and flames. It was a common trope of Renaissance thought to interpret these as symbols of spiritual realities having no physical form.

168. Continuous number answers the question "how much?" Discrete number answers the question "how many?"

In this way the whole universe may be figurated; effort is required merely for assigning subjects and adjects, choosing things that have been remembered, and assigning them their places in the chambers of the inner senses.

Of Practice with Things Conceived by Complex Terms

Just as complexity in thought or speech is made out of substantives by a copula,[169] each simple thing is compounded with another simple thing, or each of these may be divided from the other. Thus in inward writing, in which such combinations follow and are meant to be effected by a first combination from simple elements, substance connects to substance, accident is adapted to accident, the nonexistent with that in which it does not exist, the assisting to that which it assists, and the circumstantial to that which connects it to the thing of which it is a circumstance.

Such complexity appears first in the ordinary definition of the images, figures, and signs that are to be formed (leaving out the things that are enumerated with other intentions in definitions of simple things without complexity, which are not concerned with inward writing, for this latter cannot be produced without the simplicity of simple things.) It appears secondly in forming and completing spoken words, which are said by adding one or several terms to the beginning or end of a term, or to the beginning or end of several terms. It appears a third time in ordered discourse, which is made from complex terms as a body from its own limbs, as composites are connected in the final composition. As physicists say, form descends into matter first in the composition of simple bodies, and then the simple bodies are combined into imperfect mixtures. All these simple things, such as imperfect sinews, perfect bones, and the production of perfect flesh, are called homogeneous. All these parts then go to create heterogeneous members, as when they join together in the arm or the head. Ultimately all the members come together as a unity to form a living body.

Subjects and adjects are the same way, proceeding from the formation of simple things to the first combination, from that to the second, from that to the third, and thence to others, in order to make combinations up to the capacity of the substances we have set forth. For if a combination be so great and integral that it cannot take a subject, let the first combination unite subject with subject, or connect subjects with subjects; to these adjects are then added, applying

---

169. A word such as "and."

them to the things to which they should be applied. In the same way, you join one ship to another successively to form a bridge, and cross the Hellespont with dry feet.[170]

---

170. The Hellespont is the strait that connects the Mediterranean with the Black Sea, and the Persian army, when it invaded Greece, built a pontoon bridge across the Hellespont in the way Bruno describes.

A Brief and Expedited Art
To the same most Christian
King of France

An Enigma and Paradigm
by Giordano Bruno of Nola

Urania led the prophet into sublime rooms
    For the clouds of his mind were an offering to her,
Pregnant with order that is disposed in a circle
    She indicates the extent of each one with her hand.
Here sits the kingdom of Leucadia and sad old age.[171]
    Here is displayed the passing of these paternal reigns.
Next strong Mars seizes them by the spear and keeps hold of them.
    Next the golden Titan[172] makes the day.
Next sweet Venus by means of love graciously leads many to her.
    Next is the arbiter of blessed peace and of arms.
Next Lucina cries out, inconstant of face and light,
    They see her rising while lying down,[173] and waxing.
The palaces of heaven are ordered according to the image,
    Two sixes of them help those who wander through the houses.
You go forth, old man, and arise beneath a variety of places

---

171. This and the next six lines refer to the seven planets in order from Saturn to the Moon.

172. Helios, the Titan of the Sun.

173. When the Moon has just risen early in the first quarter, the two points of the crescent point toward the Earth, and so she is said to be lying face down.

As they turn; varied notes by winding together;
Thence rises the father of the gods. Gradivus[174] rises.
The Sminthæan god.[175] Cnidia,[176] born of the sea.
The nephew of Atlas rises, the son of Cyllene.[177]
Nor do you stop Delia,[178] potent in heaven and hell.

A Partial Explanation of the Enigma

 HUS, MOST SERENE KING, historians with regard to their discipline can very easily collate those things they need to keep in
memory in an orderly fashion (for example, distinguished by
volume, book, and chapter), just as though they were leading
them out of their houses into the courtyard; and in various
subjects of this kind, a variety of lives and deeds in succession, infallibly and in
a brief interval of time, being conceived before the eyes, they are put in order.

For this purpose, take the history more famous than all others, that is, of
Adam, Abel, Ham, Noah, Abraham, Isaac, Jacob, Joseph, and Moses, and constitute in the mind a house for each of them. Then use all of them in order, or
make each one the beginning of its own path; making a single room with all of
them together, or each one in its own room; following the order of historical
subjects, in order to retain the order of accidents of the universe.

In the same way, orators will be able to put the parts of an oration under
their headings. Legal scholars will put titles under books, laws under titles,
paragraphs under laws, and under these, subheadings. Physicians will put sections under laws, and chapters, parts of chapters, and aphorisms with all their
applications, in the same order that they are found in books.

It is just the same with all other things (more so than the industriousness
of the ignorant believes to be possible): they may be adapted to the material
proper to each profession.

---

174. A name of Mars.

175. A title of Apollo.

176. A name of Venus.

177. Both these are titles of Mercury.

178. A name of the Moon.

As a type of such an art, you have the following fecund figure, which can be referred to innumerable uses. In this, the constant scale of the seven planets is indicated by their characters. These may be placed around the center of a solid sphere, or around the center of a two-dimensional circle; different things are assigned to different circles, or by proceeding around portions of a single circle.

⊹

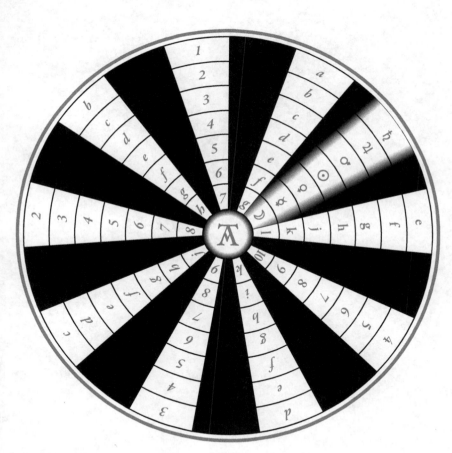

Fig. 25. The Fecund Figure

Another Brief Art

By which things of diverse orders may be referred to
their proper orders, and more forcefully remembered,
in which other arts are shown to be weak

An Enigma and Paradigm
by Giordano Bruno of Nola

The wandering might ought not to stray from the clear light,
    Nor the senses, as they run, fall behind what they follow,
And deceive you, who have been sent into the depths of Tartarus,
    Fleeing burning thirst, seeking the wave.
Powerful Circe shall bring you help in seven chambers
    In each of which species and genus carry out their actions;
Cross these fallen ones to the field of the ancient Father.
    These are born with Jove's Ganymede,
And standing with shining lights, glowering Mars
    This garden overlooks, and cruel Mulciber.[179]
You will obtain lamps renowned over the vast earth
    Where they will survey your manifold progeny.
Sweetly breathing Venus who conquers all living things
    And, being a goddess, holds them in a place set apart.
And the mystery you should trust, the herald of the gods,

---

179. A name of Vulcan.

Believed to be a woman by women, a man by men.[180]
That which is divided by many (that they shall not fear your gift),
Is united for your comfort by laborious Delia.

A Partial Explanation of the Enigma

 HIS ART PRACTICED ALL BY ITSELF will go very far, especially for those who are adept in the rotation of the wheels.
The general of an army writes notes to his centurions, in
person or through his subordinate officers, sending each his
proper orders. You ought to do the same here, using varied and
appropriate actions, passions, or circumstances, in places next to one another,
multiplied in numerical order so that you may see them inwardly with the eye of
the imagination. In this way Circe the healer quickly and effortlessly inscribed
and fixed in memory all the qualities of every herb, along with the degrees of
their qualities.[181] In the same way a schoolteacher will be able to teach students
to retain the declension of every noun (understanding by this what is properly
signified by the noun) in a single day.

Pay attention to what we have said about what is properly signified, because
opinion consists of many different names for the same thing in the same language, which are then divided under a diversity of headings. It is no wonder
that for a very long time we did not try to write sentences in memory; there are
so many different ways of saying something that all, as it is said, carry different
emphasis; just as we do not understand exactly the same thing by the words
"tunic," "clothing," and "garment."

Synonyms being thus excluded, nothing in this or any similar system gives
us trouble. Here the astrologer is able to memorize forty-eight constellations
of heaven in the four parts of the sky, together with their meaning, situation,
position, and their smallest parts (which are the stars of notable magnitude),
all related together in four chambers. Similarly, all other sciences, arts and practices, whether they have an order of their own or need ordering, may be referred
to their proper tens, hundreds, and thousands.

---

180. Mercury, who is a hermaphrodite in Renaissance alchemical lore.

181. In Renaissance medicine, each herb was held to have two qualities—warm or cold, and moist
or dry—each of which was present in one of four degrees, from one (mild) to four (extreme).

All this is shown in material form in the following scheme of twelve houses.

‡

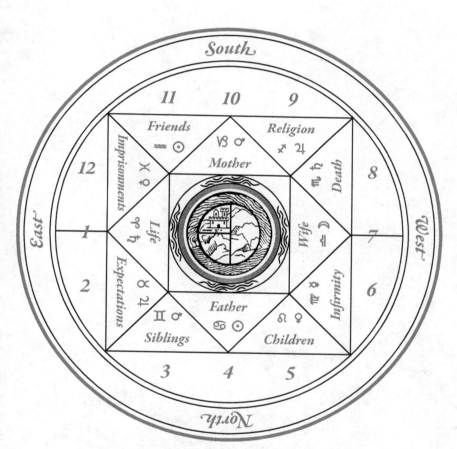

Fig. 26. *The Twelve Houses of the Circle of the Heavens*

Yet Another Brief Art
For remembering words and things

An Enigma
implying very clever subjects and forms
of an art that is worth choosing

In motion the mover, compelled by itself,
    Gives motion that proceeds with eternal immobility.
The force circling the center is understood as one
    Gyre, which is never able to cease;
And forever circling around its turning axis,
    Nor does it proceed in a straight manner.
The sage will not vary in doing the works of Nature;
    The principle remains, nor will it ever otherwise.
Proteus son of Neptune,[182] in the vast Carpathian sea,
    On his two feet drives horses after the filthy herd.
These are preserved while all forms are drawn together,
    And driven into the presence of the great gods forever on high.
Never changing, in all that is governed by Nature,
    It shows itself forever and thus is governed by the Monad.
You see that nothing denies its action to those that are beneath,
    From whence more officiously come all things.
They whirl in the chaos of Anaxagoras,[183] and they have the father

---

182. Proteus: a Greek demigod who could change himself into any shape.

183. The Greek philosopher Anaxagoras taught that air or chaos was the principle of all things.

Of the atoms of Democritus; Plato's substance is theirs.[184]
In that which receives, preserves, warns, organizes, and stores seeds,
The mother is consulted, nor without the father's intentions
Does it assist in due order to extend τῶν μικροκόσμων[185]
Which has the greatest orb enclosed in it.

Let animate subjects be in subjects in animation, and fixed in place, so that they do not move from one place to another.

Let inanimate subjects have five different places so that mute animals can make sounds.

Let there be for each animate subject instruments of twenty-four or thirty kinds, which may be applied to each of the aforesaid five different places, for the requirement and necessity of expressing what is to be expressed.

Let it be sufficient to you, though, to have each subject emit one sound. We will allow experts, to be sure, and those who have reflected with proper seriousness, to work boldly with many subjects, rather than hesitantly working with fewer in fear.

The instruments shall be of four kinds. The first are those that can go left or right. The second kind goes upward, the third goes downward, and the fourth, turning all around, perfects the rational animal.[186]

I believe therefore that it will be easy, and a very effective trick, to give each of the aforementioned five differences its own permanent instrument, so that they may be moved as new species appear.

To indicate medial letters,[187] show something in a certain place when making the form so that it will signify *L, R,* or *N.*

For final letters, let others be chosen, which you may use as terminations in Latin, Greek, Italian, Spanish, and French: *B P M L R S N C T G D F A E I Y O U.*

---

184. Atoms were the basic principles of all things according to the Greek philosopher Democritus; in the thought of Plato, abstract substance had the same role.

185. Greek, *tōn mikrokosmōn,* "the microcosm."

186. That is to say, it rotates like a human head on its neck. The head was said to "perfect the rational animal," that is, the human being.

187. That is, one of the three letters L, N, or R, that can be put in the middle of a word between one consonant vowel pair and another in Latin.

Other arts of memory have animals wander, while instruments remain; it is indeed better to do these the other way around.

Furthermore, if you find animate images more memorable than inanimate subjects when exactness is necessary, why not have several animals of the same kind (provided that their places are next to one another) to represent the thought, and then put the same combination in the same order in other places?

Thus as you proceed through different regions, it will be even easier for you to use the same things as adjects than it is with words.

Another Mode of the Art

If you wish to assign actions to animate subjects frequently or perpetually, for things to be explained opportunely, take a hundred instruments, or their results, or concomitants, or movements, or disturbances, or retreats, or events, and it may work well for you.

Enigma and Paradigm
Teaching how to assign to insensible letters the necessary forms and numbers of sensation

**This opens the hidden way
to innumerable other ways of doing things
if the unique application is perceived**

If you watch the east, another redness here surges up.
    First to appear are the faces of the Sun's horses,
Making different sounds, they look toward where setting
    The Moon shows you the heels of her horses.
The sounds are not similar where, observing watchful Bootes,
    The Nolan[188] stands alone by day and night.
It is not the same at all where the Earth, with its dense body
    Opposing the light, casts its shadow upon you.
Five different speeches he utters then, not hiding them
    In himself as he sets down everything that he knows.
But if his voice reaches the rocky cave,
    By reflected waves of air the sound is to be returned,
As the voice resounds to you. If you should put it to use,
    It returns toward the letters as a reversed note.

---

188. Bruno, of course.

Fig. 27.

Working Bruno's Magic
A Practical Guide

John Michael Greer

THE MODERN READER who approaches Bruno's *On the Shadows of the Ideas* as a manual for practice has to overcome two hurdles. The first of these, and the more obvious of the two, is the differences between the content of ordinary education in Bruno's time and ours. Many of the concepts Bruno references in this book—the categories of Aristotelian logic, for example, or the principles of astrology—were common knowledge in his time, the sort of thing that anyone who knew enough Latin to read *On the Shadows of the Ideas* in the original would know as a matter of course. Most of these concepts, in turn, are known only to specialists today. Even a basic guide to all the branches of knowledge Bruno references in this book would be considerably longer than the book itself. I have contented myself with footnotes to clarify such points as will help make sense of the text. Those readers who wish to go further should start with a general guide to the Renaissance worldview such as C.S. Lewis' *The Discarded Image*, and then proceed to more specialized historical studies.

The second hurdle that has to be leaped is less obvious than the first to a casual glance, but even more pervasive and challenging once an attempt is made to practice Bruno's methods. In our time it's a basic presupposition that knowledge should be available to all. Books that claim to teach complicated subjects to complete beginners, or for that matter complete idiots, are all over bookstore shelves; the notion that important teachings ought to be restricted to the few is deeply offensive to many people, and the associated notion that potential students should be forced to earn access to a teaching by deciphering a deliberately obscure presentation is very nearly unthinkable in today's educational climate.

Chronocentrism—the notion that the values of one particular period in time, usually the present, are superior to those of all other periods and should be used indiscriminately to pass judgment on all previous thought[189]—is epidemic in today's intellectual culture. Thus the mere fact that Giordano Bruno didn't live in our time, and so didn't share the unquestioned presuppositions of our intellectual culture, isn't always enough to remind modern readers that he can't be expected to follow the habits we consider appropriate.

Be that as it may, *On the Shadows of the Ideas* resembles nothing so much as one of the complicated fortifications that surrounded the Italian cities of Bruno's time. Some parts of it—the suburbs, so to speak, of its mental geography—are defended only by vulnerable outworks and can easily be stormed by a determined attacker. Other parts of it, including the city proper, have high walls and strong garrisons in the way of assault, and the citadel at the heart of the city rises stark and indomitable over all.

The suburbs, to unpack the metaphor a little, are the introductory arts of memory appended to *On the Shadows of the Ideas*. The city itself is Bruno's fully developed art of memory, and the citadel is the combinatorial art at the center of his entire system, which is presented in *On the Shadows of the Ideas* only in a sidelong and deliberately incomplete way.

1. The Combinatorial Art

From the thirteenth century, when Ramon Lull created the first version of the ars combinatoria, to the eighteenth, when it was abandoned and erased by European intellectual culture, scholars across Europe pursued the project of crafting an algebra of basic concepts by which philosophical questions could be settled with the certainty of mathematics. Lull argued that his system's nine absolute dignities—goodness, greatness, duration, power, wisdom, will, virtue, truth, and glory—and nine relative predicates—difference, concordance, contrariety, beginning, middle, end, majority, equality, and minority—were not only the basic constituents of logic, they were equally basic to the universe that

---

189. Chronocentrism is precisely parallel to ethnocentrism, the belief that the values of one the values of one particular society are superior to those of all other societies and should be used indiscriminately to pass judgment on the ideas and customs of every other society.

human logic sought to understand. By combining those concepts in a systematic way, he claimed, it would be possible to know all things on the basis of first principles.

Lull's original system had plenty of followers in Bruno's time, but there were alternate versions that used a greater number of basic concepts in the hope of rendering the basic system more complete. To the extent that its nature can be sorted out from the hints Bruno provides, his system—written down completely only in the pages of his lost *Clavis Magna* or *Great Key*—used sixty basic concepts, thirty drawn from Platonic philosophy and thirty taken from the Aristotelian school, and probably assigned them to the sixty terms of the Zodiac. The wheel of the Zodiac with each sign divided into its five terms was Bruno's "memory palace," the framework into which all other aspects of his mnemonic system related, while the two sets of thirty concepts were also assigned to his wheel of thirty characters, where they combined in the same way as the dignities and predicates of the Lullian art.

Any of my readers who happen to have a passionate interest in Renaissance Platonist and Aristotelian studies, and wish to use Bruno's system exactly as he devised it, now know as much about the system of the *Clavis Magna* as anyone has since Bruno's death in 1600. It may well be possible, by combing the literature of Italian Renaissance philosophical pedagogy, to figure out which thirty concepts from each of the two dominant schools of philosophy Bruno meant to apply to each of the places of his system. I lack the background to attempt this, and so will leave it as Bruno did, for those who feel the call to seek out the inmost sanctuaries of his system.

Bruno, like other philosophers of his time, believed that it was possible to construct a combinatorial system based on the fundamental patterns of existence itself, as he and they believed those patterns to be identical to the fundamental patterns of human thought. The quest for such a structure inevitably foundered on the gap between human understanding and the cosmos we attempt to understand—a gap that saw only fitful exploration in Western philosophy until the century following Bruno's death. The combinatorial art Bruno practiced, however, still has relevance even though its more ambitious hopes turned out to be misplaced.

Any set of suitably basic concepts, combined and analyzed using methods like the one Lull used, gives rise to an effective framework for learning that can be applied freely to any subject of study. Three centuries after Bruno's time, another scholar of curious lore—the French occultist Éliphas Lévi—noted this in a famous passage:

> [T]he Tarot is a true oracle, and responds to all possible questions with more clarity and infallibility than the android[190] of Albertus Magnus, to such an extent that a prisoner without any books could, in a few years, if he had only a Tarot deck and knew how to use it, acquire universal knowledge, and would speak of everything with a learning without equal and with an inexhaustible eloquence. This wheel is the true key to the notory art[191] and the Great Art of Ramon Lull; it is the true secret of the transmutation of darkness into light, it is the first and the most important of all the arcana of the Great Work."[192]

This passage has been quoted countless times in occult literature since Lévi's time, but its implications have been missed far more often than not. The prisoner Lévi imagines would not gain his universal knowledge by using the Tarot deck for divination. Instead, as the last sentence of the passage just cited makes plain, Lévi grasped the Renaissance vision of a universal method for learning, and recognized in the meanings of the Tarot trumps a set of basic categories of thought well suited to that purpose.

The 22 trumps of the Tarot can thus be used, as Lévi suggests, as the basic concepts of a combinatorial system along the same lines Bruno sketches out in *On the Shadows of the Ideas*. Those readers interested in doing so may find the proposed attributions on the following table useful. To make the alphabetical dimension work, I have assigned 22 English letters to the Tarot trumps: this is easily done by combining C and K, I and J, and U, V, and W into single letters.[193] Each letter then stands for one Tarot trump, and for the philosophical and esoteric meanings assigned to that trump. Of course the Tarot is far from

---

190. A brass head inhabited by a spirit which could supposedly answer any question.

191. A nearly forgotten branch of medieval magic. Practitioners contemplated complex figures (*notæ* in Latin) and recited incantations in order to assist them in learning various branches of scholarship.

192. Éliphas Lévi, *Doctrine and Ritual of High Magic*, trans. John Michael Greer and Mark Antony Mikituk (New York: Tarcher, 2017), p. 401.

193. Please note that these letter attributions, like Bruno's, are purely for ease of reference and are not meant to be used in the letter-by-letter analysis practiced by Cabalists, for example.

the only option along these lines, and readers who prefer some other basis for their combinatorial system may certainly follow their own inspiration.[194]

A SAMPLE TAROT-BASED COMBINATORIAL SYSTEM

	TRUMP	LETTER	CONCEPT	QUESTION
0	The Fool	A	Existence	Whether?
I	The Magician	B	Essence	What?
II	The Priestess	C/K	Context	In what?
III	The Empress	D	Origin	From what?
IV	The Emperor	E	Will	To what?
V	The Hierophant	F	Purpose	For what?
VI	The Lovers	G	Cooperation	With what?
VII	The Chariot	H	Instrumentality	By means of what?
VIII	Strength	I/J	Conflict	Against what?
IX	The Hermit	L	Isolation	Distinct from what?
X	The Wheel of Fortune	M	Sequence	Through what?
XI	Justice	N	Magnitude	How much?
XII	The Hanged Man	O	Quantity	How many?
XIII	Death	P	Limit	How far?
XIV	Temperance	Q	Duration	How long?
XV	The Devil	R	Subordination	Subjected by what?
XVI	The Tower	S	Closure	Defined by what?
XVII	The Star	T	Direction	Oriented by what?
XVIII	The Moon	U/V/W	Uncertainty	Confused by what?
XIX	The Sun	X	Completion	Fulfilled by what?
XX	Judgment	Y	Assessment	Judged by what?
XXI	The World	Z	Consequence	Followed by what?

The point of the combinatorial system, whatever its alphabet of concepts might be, is to provide a framework for thought and learning. A practitioner of

---

194. I have found, for example, that the sixteen figures of geomancy—a method of divination much practiced in the Renaissance—also provide a very functional basis for a combinatorial system along Lullist lines. See John Michael Greer, *The Art and Practice of Geomancy* (York Beach, ME: Weiser Books, 2009) for an overview of geomancy's history and practice.

Lull's classic system begins by learning the nine dignities, and recognizing that everything that exists has them—a rock, let's say, is good for something (goodness); it has a certain size (greatness) and lifespan (duration); it can do certain things (power), it can teach certain things (wisdom), and it is desirable by some beings for some reasons (will); its qualities mesh together in certain ways (virtue), some things are true about it (truth), and it achieves certain ends (glory).

Each of the nine relative predicates apply to each of the dignities—the goodness of a rock, for example, is different from the goodness of other things; it is concordant with the goodness of some things and contrary to the goodness of others, and so on. Then ten questions come into play. Is the rock good? What is its goodness? Of what does its goodness consist? Why is it good? What is the quantity of its goodness? What is the quality of its goodness? When is it good? Where is it good? How does it do good? With what does it do good?

In the same way, the sample combinatorial system sketched out here combines 22 basic predicates with 22 questions. Choose a subject for consideration, take one of the predicates—say, F, Purpose—and then ask each of the questions in turn: whether the thing you're considering has a purpose, what the purpose is, in what context does the purpose have meaning, from what does the purpose derive, to what is the purpose directed, and so on; by the time you've asked and answered each of those questions, you have a very good understanding of the purpose of the subject you've chosen.

All this seems very labored at first glance, but that's because it expresses a habit of thought unfamiliar to the modern mind and actively discouraged by modern education. Experienced practitioners of a combinatorial system such as Lull's don't have to plod step by step through such a listing of concepts and questions. When they encounter a set of ideas or engage in debate, they can speed through the familiar relationships and spot at a glance the concepts that haven't been taken into account and the questions that haven't been asked. When they work out their own arguments or ideas, they can look at each point from a galaxy of different perspectives that might never come to mind without the help of the combinatorial system and the mental training it provides. Like the Lullian adepts of the Renaissance, they supplemented the natural capacities of their minds with the systematic practices of the combinatorial art. This, in turn, the art of memory seeks to do with the natural capacities of the human memory.

2. Basic Arts of Memory

While the combinatorial system of the *Clavis Magna* is communicated only in hints, the mnemonic system Bruno derives from it is given in detail in this book. It's not a system for beginners, though. At the time when Bruno wrote, after all, most educated people had been taught the art of memory in the course of their education, and this was in addition to the constant use of rote memorization as an ordinary part of life. Every Christian in Renaissance Europe had by heart, as a matter of course, the basic creeds and prayers of the Church, and it was quite common even for lay Christians to have all one hundred fifty psalms memorized; Latin was taught to schoolchildren by rote memorization of grammatical paradigms and passages of Latin literature, starting off small and extending to lengthy texts. Modern educational theories generally condemn the use of rote memorization as a learning tool, but methods based on these same modern theories have not exactly worked well in practice, and a case can be made that the Renaissance attitude is at least worth a second look.

Be that as it may, the modern student of the art of memory who has not already practiced simpler forms of the art will have some catching up to do. The three simple forms of the art of memory Bruno appends to his more complex system (pages 145–158) are workable for this purpose, but complete beginners will find it helpful to experiment with the most basic and traditional form of the art of memory: imagining the inside of a room, with objects to be remembered placed at assigned locations in it.

Begin with a single room you know well, perhaps in your own home. Practice imagining it in detail, as though you were standing in it and turning around. Once you can do this readily, choose five places in it where memory images can be stored. Here you might find a chair, there a desk, next the top of a low bookshelf, after that the top of a filing cabinet, and finally a bare corner of the floor: places of these sorts are suitable. Look at them in your imagination one at a time, and always in the same order, until you can do that without difficulty.

Now your memory system is ready to use for simple tasks. Let's say you need to stop at the convenience store on the way home from work and pick up a few things. In your imagination, place each of the things on your shopping list in one of the five places—the box of sugar on the chair, the carton of milk on the desk, the double order of broasted chicken on top of the bookshelf, and so on. When you get to the store, you'll find that the images are still waiting in your imagination, exactly where you left them.

A little experimentation with this method will quickly demonstrate just how dramatically the art of memory assists the natural ability to remember. With regular practice, the single room with five memory places in it can be expanded by the addition of other rooms. Practitioners in the ancient world and the Renaissance routinely had whole memory palaces, sometimes modeled on actual buildings, sometimes freely invented, in which memory images were stored for recall. The popular treatises of the time had standard rules—the memory rooms should be imagined as well lit, the places for images should not be crammed close together or spaced too far apart, and so on. Imagine a Renaissance scholar or mage sitting in a tapestried room, eyes closed, while walking in imagination through an ornate structure full of vivid images, each of which recalls some piece of knowledge: that habit was a commonplace of Giordano Bruno's time.

The popular memory treatises of Bruno's time drew an important distinction between memory for things and memory for words. The first of these is by far the easier of the two; even if the things you are trying to remember are highly complex and abstract, they can be represented by striking visual images that cling to the memory. Puns, exaggerations, visual clichés, bad jokes, the outrageous, the offensive, and the absurd—all these are fair game in constructing images. Thus, to invent a few modern examples, a medical student who wanted to remember a list of symptoms of streptococcus infection might start off with an image of someone fastened with canvas straps to a rotting carcass (strapped-to-carcass = streptococcus), while an astrologer who wanted to memorize a chart that had, among other aspects, Mars inconjunct Neptune might put the images of the Roman gods Mars and Neptune sitting together aboard a Chinese junk painted in big black and white stripes, like an old-fashioned convict's uniform (in-con-junk = inconjunct, with the traditional images of the gods standing in for the planets).

All this is relatively straightforward, and a little practice will make it a quick and efficient way to memorize large amounts of information and recall it accurately. The difficulty comes in when what has to be memorized consists of specific passages of text rather than concepts. If the passage is of any length, coming up with a unique image for each word rapidly becomes a burden, and it's far too easy to lose details amid the heaps of verbiage. Simply piling together images for individual letters, in turn, becomes immensely cumbersome in short order.

This is the problem that Bruno's innovations are meant to solve. He noted that in Latin—the language of scholarship in the Europe of his time—most words are composed of consonant-vowel pairs, and so a set of images corresponding to each such pair can be assembled, along with a set of images for single letters, to make memorable images for words. Consider the opening line of Caesar's Commentaries on the Gallic War: *Gallia est omnis divisa in partes tres* ("All Gaul is divided into three parts"). Bruno would divide that as GA-LI-A[195] EST OM-NI-S DI-VISA IN PA-R-TE-S T-RE-S: that is, 18 pairs or single letters instead of 31 individual letters. He would then make one of these pairs in each word a figure—for example, in Gallia, GA would become the figure of Husbal, the inventor of the process of roasting lime to make cement. To recall the identity of this figure, Bruno might have put him in workman's costume with a shovel full of quicklime in his hands. LI, drawing an image from another of Bruno's lists, would be represented by having Husbal's hair on fire; Bruno doesn't give images for individual letters, since these were a commonplace of the art of memory of his time, but we can imagine something else absurd loaded onto poor Husbal to complete the image.

One idiosyncrasy of Bruno's system is that the names of the images he gives have no relation to the sounds they express. As suggested in the introduction, this may be an adaptation to make the memory system also function as a method of cryptography. Those readers who don't need this additional function can make the process of learning a system of Bruno's type much easier by replacing his lists of names, items, and so on with lists of their own, in which the name of every person or item starts with the two letters it is meant to represent. Thus Gallia, again, could be represented by the fictional character Gandalf (= GA) with a litterbag (= LI) on his head instead of a tall pointed hat, and perhaps an anteater (= A) staring bemusedly up at him from the ground behind him.

The key to using this method is to have your images for letter pairs and single letters ready for use and committed to memory, and to have multiple images— say, one assortment of primary figures (such as Gandalf for GA), several other assortments of items that can be added to the primary figures (such as the litterbag for LI), and a list or two of images of single letters. Bruno's point about sitting and standing figures should be applied here as well—thus Gandalf, say, would represent GA when standing and AG when seated.

---

195. Doubled letters, like U after Q, can be dispensed with so long as this does not lead to confusion. The point of the image is to stimulate the memory, not to copy mechanically.

This is equally useful in English, which uses consonant-vowel pairs only a little less relentlessly than Latin. Consider a word such as "agriculture," which can be turned into five pairs and a single letter (AG, RI, CU, L, TU, RE) and assembled into a single image—say, Gandalf (GA) sitting (converting his meaning to AG) in a rickshaw (RI) with a cummerbund (CU) draped over his head, while Elmer Fudd (L) marches behind the rickshaw playing a tuba (TU) and wearing huge red (RE) shoes. (The rickshaw may be pulled by a figure representing the previous word.)

It's useful to have some obvious distinction between figures representing letter pairs such as AG, and figures representing single letters such as L. In the example just given, letter pairs representing subjects are drawn from characters in fantasy fiction such as Gandalf, while single letters representing subjects are drawn from characters in old cartoons such as Elmer Fudd. This makes it easier to remember that Mr. Fudd stands for the letter L rather than the letter pair EL (which in this example might be Elrond).

In Bruno's simple versions of the art of memory, these figures are placed into one of several schemes. The first of them uses a sequence of nine characters from the Old Testament—Adam, Abel, Ham, Noah, Abraham, Isaac, Jacob, Joseph, and Moses—to provide the overall ordering of the rooms of a memory palace. Each figure can have a room assigned to him, with five places for memory images in the room; with practice, the mind moves easily from room to room, recognizing each room by the Biblical figure who appears in it and seeing the memory images in their proper places around it.

This same principle, Bruno points out, can be used with anything else that forms an order easy to memorize, such as the sequence of chapters in a book. Within any given division, furthermore, the same principle can be applied to produce a kind of outline structure, in which the rememberer goes to the room representing a volume, say, then from there chooses the room representing a chapter, then to the subchapter, then to the section and subsection, so that each passage of memorized text is recalled in its proper place, and can be called to mind almost instantly when required.

His second scheme uses nested repetitions of a single figure, rather than varying the arrangement to fit the material that needs to be memorized. The example he gives is the standard astrological map of the twelve houses. Each house contains, in turn, a figure of twelve houses, each of these subdivisions a figure of twelve houses, and so on through as many iterations as necessary to provide enough places for whatever is to be memorized.

A third scheme starts by memorizing a series of images so linked that the mind easily passes from one to the next—for example, the signs of the zodiac. Each image has five places on it where some object representing a letter or pair of letters can be placed. Thus, to continue the example, Aries the Ram has an object on its head, one on its neck, one on the ground before its feet, one on its forequarters and one on its hindquarters; Taurus the Bull has the same set of places; Gemini the Twins have one object on each head, one around each neck, and one hanging from their joined hands, and so on. So long as a convenient set of symbolic objects to represent letters has been committed to memory, this method will allow short passages of text to be memorized almost instantly— and of course the same principle can be applied to many more than twelve images.

Other arrangements can be devised as needed. That, of course, is one of the central themes of Bruno's work. In place of the formulaic arts of memory offered by most writers on the subject, he offered a set of basic principles and a cascade of schemes for applying them. His later books *Ars Reminiscendi ("The Art of Remembering")* and *Explicatio Triginti Sigillorum ("Explanation of the Thirty Sigils")*, both published the year after *On the Shadows of the Ideas*, amplify this point by providing thirty different patterns in which memory images can be arranged for ease of recollection. The adaptation of the arrangement of memory images to the topics to be memorized, at the same time, is the bridge by which the basic forms of the art of memory Bruno presents make the transition to his fully realized art of memory—an art by which, at least in principle, all existing knowledge could be arranged in a single vast pattern of images and then, following the rules of the combinatorial art, used as the basis for contemplations that would reveal everything that could be known by the human mind.

3. The Whole Art of Memory

Barring the discovery of previously unpublished documents, Bruno's fully developed art of memory is probably beyond recovery. Certain things, though, can be known about it. The basis of that art, as already noted, is a single memory image, probably the circle of the zodiac with each sign divided into its five terms, and with fundamental concepts from Platonic and Aristotelian philosophy assigned to each term.

In Bruno's time, the leading intellectuals of the age hoped to understand the basic architecture of reality, which they conflated with the basic architecture of human thought; they believed, as a result of that conflation, that it was possible to reduce all human knowledge to a natural order that would allow every least detail to be traced back to one of the essential principles of existence; and they hoped that once all existing knowledge was arranged in terms of its natural order, it would be possible to proceed the other way, starting from first principles, and understand the entire universe and everything in it.

For most sixteenth- and seventeenth-century attempts toward that supremely ambitious project, some version of Ramon Lull's combinatorial art provided the ground plan, while arts of memory that derived from a Lullist set of dignities or principles in one way or another provided the raw material from which the practitioner attempted to assemble his universal knowledge. Bruno's version, elaborate as it was, followed this scheme precisely. Lacking exact knowledge of the concepts that Bruno applied to his wheel of thirty letters to create the combinatorial system he used, it's unlikely that the precise shape of Bruno's fully developed mnemonics can be worked out, but a few things can be known or guessed from Bruno's own hints.

To begin with, Bruno moved beyond the rigid distinction between places and figures that played so central a role in the traditional art of memory. In place of architectural settings, real or otherwise, Bruno's full method made use of sequences of images that were linked to one another so that each led naturally to the next. Several passages in the text suggest that the linkages that bound one image to the next were meant to mirror the parallel linkages between real things in the universe, so that the flow of ideas followed the natural patterns of existence—at least in theory. The adjects or additional images added to each primary image served, at minimum, as a label to recall the proper name of the subject, and from each image other strings of images went cascading outward, descending from general to specific concepts and from abstractions to concrete examples, ending in passages of text committed to memory using Bruno's methods.

The result of this method in practice must have been a little like an internal, vividly imagined version of Giulio Camillo's memory theater, one of the great intellectual projects of the sixteenth century.[196] Camillo's theater was an actual structure of wood, semicircular like a Roman amphitheater, with seven levels rising from the front to the back and seven gangways rising through the levels; each gangway and each level was attributed to one of the seven planets; where each gangway crossed each level there was a gate rich with symbolic ornamentation, and beside each gate were drawers containing written texts, taken from the writings of Cicero, on subjects relevant to the themes indicated by the gate. Though the fine details of Camillo's system are as obscure as those of Bruno's, it seems to have functioned as a sort of symbolic memory bank and filing system, in which anyone who knew the secret could quickly find a cogent response to any conceivable question.

In the same way, Bruno—like many of his contemporaries—hoped to construct an architecture of memory that would contain the entire body of human knowledge. The adept of Bruno's system, starting from the sixty basic concepts of his primary image, would gradually build up an immense collection of linked images designed to call to mind all the basic concepts of every field of human knowledge available to Renaissance Europe, from theology and philosophy through such practical fields of medicine and law. That was the goal of the pansophic intellectual movements of the time, and the system Bruno expounded in his lost *Great Key* and sketched out in teasing hints in *On the Shadows of the Ideas* was arguably the closest approach to that ideal that any of the minds of the Renaissance achieved.

Looking back across four centuries separating the present time from Bruno's day, the goal of the Renaissance pansophists may seem absurd. Much of the reason for that apparent absurdity, though, is that the sum of available knowledge has increased explosively since the end of the Middle Ages. Not that many centuries before Bruno's time, after all, it was entirely possible for a single mind to grasp the entire landscape of accepted knowledge available to the scholars of the time. During the Renaissance, it was still just reasonable to imagine this as a possibility, before the great age of European exploration and the first achievements of the scientific revolution began to push the boundaries of the known far beyond the limits of any one mind. Thereafter, the creators of systems focused on specific branches of knowledge—Carl von Linné's great *System of*

---

196. See the description in Frances Yates, *The Art of Memory* (Chicago: University of Chicago Press, 1966), pp. 135–162.

Nature, first published in 1735 and still the basis of classification in the life sciences today, is a case in point.

Yet the vision of a method for correlating disparate fields of knowledge using an abstract structure linked to fundamental philosophical concepts remains valid, and potentially useful, in other contexts. Nobel Prize-winning author Hermann Hesse, in his last and most intricate novel *Das Glassperlenspiel* (*"The Glass Bead Game,"* 1945), drew on his own knowledge of Renaissance and early modern pansophic schemes to reimagine such a system as an art form and a spiritual discipline. In much the same way, Éliphas Lévi's revisioning of the Renaissance magical tradition gave rise to modern occult traditions in which cascading correspondences from many traditions form the basis of a symbolic alphabet as intricate as anything Bruno ever devised. The central vision at the heart of Bruno's work thus remains worth exploring, and when the contemporary fetishization of technology gives way to a new appreciation for the capacities of the trained human mind, as it doubtless will in time, it's entirely possible that some new manifestation of the pansophic impulse will seize the imagination of that future period as it did the imagination of the Renaissance. If Bruno's work helps pave the way toward the mnemonic and combinatorial systems of the future, that seems like a suitable memorial for its creator.

Glossary

ACCIDENT: a quality present in a substance; Renaissance philosophy commonly compared the relationship between substance and accident to that between wax and the seal pressed into it

AGENT: anything that acts on a patient; see PATIENT

ANIMA MUNDI: the soul or rational consciousness of the world, one of the central concepts of Renaissance occult philosophy

CHARACTERS: in Renaissance occult literature, magical letters (Latin CHARACTERES) which were used to summon spirits or enchant talismans

IDEA: in Renaissance Platonism, a pattern in the divine mind, imitated imperfectly by lower levels of existence

INTELLIGIBLE: capable of being perceived by the mind

GENUS: any broadly (as we still say, "generally") defined class of entity, composed of one or more species

NOTES: in Renaissance occult literature, magical diagrams (Latin *notæ*) used in the *ars notoria*, a magical art used to assist learning. Practitioners copied out *notæ* corresponding to the branch of learning they wished to master, and contemplated them while reciting an appropriate prayer

PATIENT: anything that is acted on by an agent; see AGENT

SCALE OF NATURE: the ladder (Latin *scala*) of levels of being, descending from the divine unity to formless matter

SENSIBLE: capable of being perceived by the senses

SIGILS: in Renaissance occult literature, magical seals (Latin *sigillæ*) which contained the magical power of a spirit or occult potency

SPECIES: any narrowly (as we still say, "specifically") defined class of entity, composed of one or more individuals; the goal of the art of memory is to accurately record the species of things that are to be memorized

SUBJECT: in Bruno's mnemonic terminology, the image of a person, animal or object

SUBSTANCE: something that has real existence in its own right, such as intellect, soul, or pure unformed matter

SUPERSUBSTANTIAL: the divine unity, which was held to be above existence.

TERM(S), ASTROLOGICAL: uneven divisions of the twelve signs of the Zodiac, five of which belong to each sign

References

Culianu, Ioan. *Eros and Magic in the Renaissance*. Chicago: University of Chicago Press, 1997.

de León-Jones, Karen Silvia. *Giordano Bruno and the Kabbalah: Prophets. Magicians, and Rabbis*. New Haven, CT: Yale University Press, 1997.

Greer, John Michael. *The Art and Practice of Geomancy*. York Beach, ME: Weiser Books, 2009.

Greer, John Michael, and Christopher Warnock, trans. *Picatrix: The Classic Medieval Handbook of Astrological Magic*. Iowa City, IA: Renaissance Astrology, 2010.

Hesse, Hermann. *The Glass Bead Game*. Trans. Richard and Clara Winston. New York: Holt Rinehart and Winston, 1969.

Lévi, Éliphas. *Doctrine and Ritual of High Magic*. Trans. John Michael Greer and Mark Antony Mikituk. New York: Tarcher, 2017.

Plotinus. *The Enneads*. Trans. Stephen MacKenna. Burdett, NY: Larson Publications, 1992.

Rossi, Paolo. *Logic and the Art of Memory: The Quest for a Universal Language*. Trans. Stephen Clucas. Chicago: University of Chicago Press, 2000.

Rowland, Ingrid D. *Giordano Bruno: Philosopher/Heretic*. New York: Farrar, Straus and Giroux, 2008.

Stevenson, David. *The Origins of Freemasonry*. Cambridge: Cambridge University Press, 1988.

Waterfield, Robin, trans. *The Theology of Arithmetic*. Grand Rapids, MI: Phanes, 1988.

Yates, Frances. *The Art of Memory*. Chicago: University of Chicago Press, 1966.

—, *Giordano Bruno and the Hermetic Tradition*. Chicago: University of Chicago Press, 1964.

About the Translator

JOHN MICHAEL GREER *is Grand Archdruid Emeritus of the Ancient Order of Druids in America. He is the author of more than thirty books on a wide range of subjects, including* Paths of Wisdom: Cabala in the Western Tradition *(Llewellyn, 1996);* Inside A Magical Lodge: Group Ritual in the Western Tradition *(Llewellyn, 1998);* The Art And Practice Of Geomancy: Divination, Magic, and Earth Wisdom of the Renaissance *(Weiser, 2009);* The Druid Grove Handbook: A Guide to Ritual in the Ancient Order of Druids in America *(Lorain Press, 2011);* The Gnostic Celtic Church: A Manual and Book of Liturgy *(Lorian Press, 2013); and* After Progress: Reason and Religion at the End of the Industrial Age *(New Society Publishers, 2015). With Christopher Warnock, he translated* The Picatrix: The Occult Classic of Astrological Magic *(Adocentyn Press, 2010–11). He is also the editor of the new edition of Israel Regardie's* The Golden Dawn: The Original Account of the Teachings, Rites, and Ceremonies of the Hermetic Order *(Llewellyn, 2016). He lives in Cumberland, Maryland, an old red brick mill town in the north central Appalachians, with his wife Sara. You may follow his weekly blogging at* Ecosophia: Toward an Ecological Spirituality *(www.ecosophia.net).*

⹋

About the Publisher

AZOTH PRESS *is a small independent
publishing house which makes its home in the
Pacific Northwest. Our purpose is to create
extraordinary books by practicing magicians
for the practicing magician, with a standard of
knowledge influenced by years of dedicated occult
study and magical experience. We hope that
our books will contribute to the practitioner's
evolution and transformation, and also add to
the magician's library a collection of unique,
hand-made tomes meant to last for generations.
Magical books should be Hermetic and talismanic
works of art produced by the conjunction of well-
written, well-researched, and enlightening content
with beautiful design and elegant binding. In line
with our goal of creating such magical volumes
for practitioners and scholars of the Great Work,
all Azoth Press limited-edition books are hand-
bound by artisans with decades of experience in
the fields of printing and master bookbinding.
Each book is manufactured not only to a high
æsthetic standard to please the eye and hand,
but also to a demanding standard of artisanship
and materials, so that each rare volume may be
handed down, read, and used in their practice
by generations of magicians to come. Please visit
our website at azothpress.com and follow us on
Facebook at www.facebook.com/AzothPress/.*

⁜

CPSIA information can be obtained
at www.ICGtesting.com
Printed in the USA
LVHW050251191120
672010LV00006B/303